MEAT AND OTHER LOAVES

GW00692200

MEAT AND OTHER LOAVES

by
Jeanette P. Egan

Illustrations by
Michelle Burchard

HPBooks

HPBooks
Published by The Berkley Publishing Group
200 Madison Avenue
New York, NY 10016

Copyright © 1995 by Jeanette P. Egan
Cover photography by Cormier Photography

First edition: February 1995

Published simultaneously in Canada.

Library of Congress Cataloging-in-Publication Data

Egan, Jeanette P.
    Meat and other loaves / Jeanette P. Egan.—1st ed.
        p.   cm.
    Includes index.
    ISBN 1-55788-198-7 (trade pbk. : acid-free paper)
    1. Meat loaf.   I. Title.
TX749.E34   1995
641.8'24—dc20   94-31281
                                                             CIP

Printed in the United States of America

10   9   8   7   6   5   4   3   2   1

Notice: The information printed in this book is true and
complete to the best of our knowledge. All recommendations
are made without any guarantees on the part of the author or
the publisher. The author and publisher disclaim all liability
in connection with the use of this information.

This book is printed on acid-free paper.

Contents

Introduction

When a loaf is used as a main dish, everyone immediately thinks "meatloaf" or a loaf made of a combination of beef and pork, but a loaf can be made using meat, chicken, turkey, seafood, and even vegetables as the main ingredient. In fact, all of these ingredients are used in the recipes in this cookbook.

Everyone has a favorite meatloaf recipe, but in today's search for meals with fewer calories and less fat, it's fun to be creative and think of new ways to make and serve traditional dishes.

What is a loaf? In this book we start with what is probably considered to be standard loaves of beef and pork, then rapidly take advantage of all the other possibilities of making loaves out of chicken, turkey, vegetables, nuts, beans, cheese, and eggs. Some are wrapped with pastry, others are steamed in ring molds. The only thing all the loaf recipes have in common is they have a somewhat loaf shape (and of course they taste delicious).

Most of the loaves are meant to be eaten as

main dishes accompanied by vegetables and sauces, but some even serve as both "the meat and the potato." Other loaves are equally suitable as an appetizer or a main dish. Some are best hot, but many of the loaves are wonderful cold for lunch the next day. Others practically beg you to take them on a picnic, to be served with fresh fruit, cheese, a loaf of crusty bread, a few pickles, and perhaps a glass of wine.

Main Ingredients

Meat In meat loaves the main ingredient is meat—usually beef and/or pork. The amount of fat in the meat (see chart, page 10) determines how moist the loaf will be and also how much it will shrink during cooking. For fattier meats (greater than 20 percent fat), I prefer to drain the fat off during cooking or use one of the special pans that allows the fat to drain.

Ground lamb can also be used in meatloaves, but try to get a lean grind, or pour off the fat halfway through the cooking time. Loaves are a perfect way to use leftover ham. The ham can be cut into chunks and chopped in the food processor or ground in a meat grinder.

Poultry Chicken and turkey are also available in different fat levels (see chart, page 10). The advantage of using chicken and turkey is lower amounts of fat, especially saturated fat.

Duck is also used in loaves, particularly in pâté-type loaves. Make duck loaves in pans that are specially designed to drain off the fat, or drain as needed during cooking to remove much of the fat. However, if all the fat is removed, the loaf may be dry.

Seafood Fish and shellfish can both be used in loaves, either by chopping in the food processor or by layering strips of fish and pieces of shellfish with other ingredients.

Most seafood is low in fat and needs to be combined with other ingredients to retain moisture. Usually seafood loaves that are mostly fish or shellfish are baked in a pan of water (bain marie) to prevent drying and overcooking. Often seafood loaves are steamed or poached.

Other main ingredients For those who prefer loaves made without meat, poultry, or seafood, there are beans, nuts, grains, and vegetables. In fact, very few loaves contain only meat—most are flavored by at least some of the aromatic vegetables. But nuts, grains, and vegetables can be the main ingredients instead of meat in loaves as well (and sometimes your family and friends won't know the difference).

Other Ingredients

Liquids Added liquid, in addition to the fat that may be present, makes a loaf moist, so usually tomato sauce or barbecue sauce, pureed fruits such as applesauce, milk or cream, wine or beer, or other liquids are added. Liquids also add flavor.

Eggs In addition to a liquid, eggs are often added. Egg whites or egg substitutes can be used as well and can reduce the amount of cholesterol in a loaf. Eggs help bind ingredients together. Large eggs or their equivalents were used in all recipes.

Fillers Fresh or dry bread crumbs are often added as a filler and to help the loaf stay together. Loaves in this book use crumbs, oats, couscous, cooked rice, cracker crumbs, and even corn tortillas and polenta. These ingredients add flavor, retain the juices, and make a moist loaf. A meatloaf made from all meat is very dense and firm.

Equipment

Most of these recipes require little special equipment other than that found in a well-stocked kitchen, but I would like to mention a few items that I find helpful.

Food processor This can be used for finely chopping vegetables (important in the all-vegetable loaves), grinding meat to your specifications, pureeing cooked beans, chopping nuts, and mixing ingredients together.

Meat grinder attachment for mixer If you really prefer grinding meat and poultry yourself and already have the mixer, this is an inexpensive tool to buy.

Nonstick loaf pans These are wonderful—especially for loaves that contain cheese or for those delicate vegetable loaves that tend to stick to the bottom of the pan (OOPS) when you turn them out.

Double loaf pan with holes to drain fat This is great for loaves that are made with lamb or other fatty mixtures. The fat can be poured into an empty container (never the drain) and put into the garbage.

Ground Beef

Type of beef*	Percentage of fat by weight
Ground beef	Up to 30 percent
Ground chuck	About 20 percent
Ground round	About 15 percent
Lean ground beef	About 20 percent
Extra-lean ground beef	About 10 percent

* Store brands vary, as do the percentages of fat. You can also select a cut of meat and have the butcher grind it for you.

Ground Turkey and Chicken

Type*	Percentage of fat by weight
Ground turkey contains skin	20 percent
Extra-lean ground turkey breast only, no skin	2 percent
Ground chicken contains skin	20 percent
Lean ground chicken thighs, no skin	10 percent

* Always read the label on chicken and turkey products to determine if skin is ground with the meat and also whether light or dark meat is used. The mix will vary with the brand.

Is It Done Yet?

How do you tell when a meat or other loaf is done? Ovens and pans vary. (Dark pans cook food quicker in the oven.) So even though you cooked the loaf the time given in the recipe, it may not be done or may even be overdone.

- Set the timer for 10 to 15 minutes less than the recipe says and check the loaf.
- The best and safest way to determine if the loaf is done is a thermometer. Remove loaf from oven and insert an instant-read thermometer in center of loaf. The temperature should be between 160°F (70°C) and 170°F (75°C).

Other clues include:

- The loaf has come away from the sides of the pan and is browned.
- The loaf springs back when lightly pressed.
- Juices run clear when loaf is pierced in center. Don't do this often or the loaf will be dry.

What to Do with Leftovers

- Make sandwiches—especially good when made with meat, chicken, or turkey loaves.
- Cut slices into cubes and serve as appetizers with dipping sauces.
- Cut into very thin slices and serve with a fruit salsa or other sauce as a first course.
- Freeze in individual slices and heat in the microwave for quick dinners.
- Crumble and use as a filling for tacos.
- Crumble and add to pasta sauce or pizzas.

Meat Loaves

This is where you would expect to find the traditional loaves, and find them you will. But don't expect to stop there—this chapter contains a lot more.

Loaves are made from ham, corned beef, cold cuts, and sausage, as well as ground beef, pork, and lamb. Many of the recipes contain vegetables, beans, and fruit, as well as eggs, crumbs, and herbs. Some of the loaves are filled with surprises, others are layered and stuffed.

Easy Beef Loaf

Serve with fresh salsa or Easy Tomato Sauce (page 118)
and Oven-Roasted Potato Wedges (page 116).

2 pounds lean ground beef
1/2 cup minced onion
2 garlic cloves, minced
1/4 cup dry bread crumbs
3/4 cup milk
1/2 teaspoon dried leaf basil
1/2 teaspoon dried red chile flakes (optional)
Salt and freshly ground black pepper

Preheat oven to 350°F (175°C). Spray a 13″ × 9″ baking pan with nonstick cooking spray or lightly grease.

Combine meat, onion, garlic, bread crumbs, milk, basil, pepper flakes, if using, salt, and pepper in a medium-size bowl. Using your hands or an electric mixer, mix until thoroughly combined.

Shape meat mixture into an 8″ × 4″ loaf in baking pan. Bake about 40 minutes or until juices run clear when pierced with a knife. Let stand 5 minutes, then cut into thick slices. Makes 4 to 6 servings.

Spicy Beef & Bean-filled Cornbread Loaf

You'll find many of the flavors of the Old West in this mouth-warming loaf.
If you prefer it less spicy, omit the jalapeño chile.

1 pound ground beef sirloin
1/2 cup chopped green onions
1 jalapeño chile, minced
1/2 cup plus 1 tablespoon all-purpose flour
1 cup cooked pinto beans, well drained
1 cup cornmeal
1 teaspoon baking powder
1 teaspoon salt
1/4 teaspoon baking soda
2 teaspoons chili powder
1 teaspoon ground cumin
1 cup buttermilk (see Note below)
1 egg, lightly beaten

Preheat oven to 400°F (205°C). Grease a 9″ × 5″ loaf pan. Cook beef, green onions, and jalapeño in a medium-size skillet over medium heat until browned, stirring to break up meat. Drain off excess fat. Sprinkle 1 tablespoon of the flour over meat and stir to combine; stir in beans. Set aside.

Combine cornmeal, the remaining 1/2 cup flour, baking powder, salt, soda, chili powder, and cumin in a medium-size bowl. Combine buttermilk and egg in a small bowl. Stir milk mixture into dry ingredients just until combined. Stir meat mixture into batter.

Transfer mixture to loaf pan. Bake 30 minutes or until top springs back when lightly pressed. Let stand in pan 10 minutes. Makes 4 to 6 servings.

Note

Buttermilk substitute: Add 1 tablespoon lemon juice or vinegar to a liquid measuring cup. Fill cup with milk. Let stand a few minutes.

Potato-Wrapped Beef & Beans Loaf

Beans, beef, and bourbon—the three Bs make this meatloaf one that may cause food snobs to despair, but only until the first bite. Pass the ketchup, please.

1 pound ground beef
1 (16-oz.) can pork and beans
1 cup chopped onion
1 green bell pepper, chopped
1 garlic clove, minced
1/4 cup fresh bread crumbs
1 egg
1 tablespoon chili powder
1 tablespoon dried leaf basil
1 teaspoon ground cumin
1/4 cup bourbon or water
Salt and freshly ground pepper
1 recipe Mashed Potatoes (page 114)

Preheat oven to 350°F (175°C). Spray a 15″ × 10″ baking pan with nonstick cooking spray or lightly grease.

Combine meat, pork and beans, onion, bell pepper, garlic, bread crumbs, egg, chili powder, basil, cumin, bourbon, salt, and pepper in a medium-size bowl. Using your hands or an electric mixer, mix until thoroughly combined.

Shape meat mixture into an 8-inch round loaf in baking pan. Bake about 40 minutes or until juices run clear when pierced with a knife. Cover loaf with potatoes. Increase oven temperature to 400°F (205°C). Bake until potatoes are lightly browned, about 10 minutes. Let stand 5 minutes, then cut into thick slices. Makes 4 to 6 servings.

Beef Lasagna Loaves

Forget layering meat sauce, pasta, and cheese filling—here it's all done in one bowl with no precooking except for the pasta, which should be slightly undercooked because it will continue to cook as the loaf bakes.

2 pounds lean ground beef
8 ounces ziti, cooked
2 cups cottage cheese
1/4 cup freshly grated Parmesan cheese
1 cup shredded Swiss cheese (4 ounces)
1 cup fresh chopped plum tomatoes
1 (15-oz.) can tomato sauce
1 (2-1/4-oz.) can sliced ripe olives, drained
2 eggs
2 tablespoons basil
1 teaspoon oregano
1/4 teaspoon hot chile flakes or to taste
Salt and freshly ground pepper

Preheat oven to 350°F (175°C). Spray 2 (9″ × 5″) loaf pans with nonstick cooking spray or lightly grease.

Combine meat, ziti, cheeses, tomatoes, tomato sauce, olives, eggs, basil, oregano, chile flakes, salt, and pepper in a medium-size bowl. Transfer mixture to loaf pans.

Bake about 1 hour or until loaf is firm. Let stand 5 minutes, then cut into thick slices. Makes 8 to 10 servings.

Variation

Bake one loaf and freeze the other before baking. Wrap tightly and freeze up to 1 month. Thaw overnight in refrigerator before baking.

Asparagus-Prosciutto-Stuffed Loaf

This ordinary-looking loaf is filled with a surprise.

1 pound ground beef sirloin
8 ounces bulk turkey sausage
3 tablespoons dry bread crumbs
1 egg, lightly beaten
1/4 cup apple juice
1 garlic clove, minced
1 tablespoon chopped flat-leaf parsley
Salt and freshly ground pepper
6 asparagus spears
6 slices of prosciutto

Preheat oven to 350°F (175°C). Grease an 8″ × 4″ loaf pan. Combine beef, sausage, bread crumbs, egg, apple juice, garlic, parsley, salt, and pepper in a medium-size bowl. Using your hands or an electric mixer, mix until thoroughly combined.

Transfer half of meat mixture to loaf pan. Roll asparagus in prosciutto slices. Place a row of wrapped asparagus over meat mixture, pressing asparagus slightly into meat. Top with remaining meat mixture.

Bake about 1 hour or until juices run clear when pierced with a knife. Let stand 10 minutes. Drain off any liquid. Makes 4 to 6 servings.

Sausage-stuffed Pork Loaf

Kids love it when you slice this loaf, exposing rounds of the bratwurst.

1 pound ground pork
1/2 pound ground ham
1 cup sauerkraut, drained
1/4 cup minced onion
1 tablespoon prepared mustard
1 cup fresh pumpernickel crumbs
1/2 cup beer or apple juice
1 egg, lightly beaten
1/2 teaspoon caraway seeds
1/2 teaspoon salt
Freshly ground pepper
2 cooked bratwurst

Preheat oven to 350°F (175°C). Grease a 9″ × 5″ loaf pan. Combine pork, ham, sauerkraut, onion, mustard, bread crumbs, beer, egg, caraway seeds, salt, and pepper in a medium-size bowl. Using your hands or an electric mixer, mix until thoroughly combined.

Transfer half of meat mixture to loaf pan. Place bratwurst over meat mixture, pressing bratwurst slightly into meat. Top with remaining meat mixture.

Bake about 1 hour or until juices run clear when pierced with a knife. Let stand 10 minutes. Drain off any liquid. Makes 4 to 6 servings.

Russell's Loaf

I first ate this at the dairy and fruit farm belonging to my brother, Russell. It's a hearty one-dish meal that he often feeds to farmhands and unexpected visitors.

1 pound ground beef
1/2 pound bulk turkey sausage
3/4 cup rolled oats
1 egg, lightly beaten
1 (28-oz.) can tomatoes in juice
1 teaspoon Worcestershire sauce
Dash hot pepper sauce
Salt and freshly ground pepper
4 potatoes, unpeeled, cut into 8 wedges each
2 large carrots, cut into 2-inch lengths
1 large onion, cut into thin wedges
2 celery stalks, cut into 2-inch lengths
1 teaspoon dried leaf thyme

Preheat oven to 350°F (175°C). Spray a large baking pan with nonstick cooking spray or lightly grease.

Combine beef, sausage, oats, egg, 1/2 cup juice from tomatoes, Worcestershire sauce, hot pepper sauce, salt, and pepper in a medium-size bowl. Using your hands or an electric mixer, mix until thoroughly combined.

Shape meat mixture into an oval loaf in pan. Arrange potatoes, carrots, onion, and celery around loaf. Season vegetables with salt and pepper and sprinkle with thyme. Pour tomatoes over vegetables. Cover with foil or a lid.

Bake about 1 hour, then uncover and bake 20 minutes to brown loaf and vegetables. Let stand 10 minutes, transfer vegetables to a serving bowl, and cut loaf into thick slices. Makes 6 to 8 servings.

Barbecued Beef & Potato Roll

Small wranglers don't need a second call when you prepare this beef and potato roll.

1-1/2 pounds ground beef
1/4 cup dry bread crumbs
1/4 cup minced onion
2 garlic cloves, minced
1 egg, lightly beaten
3/4 cup thick barbecue sauce
Salt and freshly ground pepper
1 cup shredded Monterey Jack cheese (4 ounces)
1 large russet potato, partially baked and shredded

Preheat oven to 350°F (175°C). Grease a 9″ × 5″ loaf pan. Combine beef, bread crumbs, onion, garlic, egg, and 1/2 cup of the barbecue sauce in a medium-size bowl. On waxed paper, pat out mixture into a 12″ × 9″ rectangle.

Spread half the cheese over meat. Top with potatoes, then remaining cheese. Roll up jellyroll style, starting at one short side and using waxed paper to help. Place seam side down in loaf pan.

Bake 1 hour. Spoon remaining barbecue sauce over loaf and bake 15 minutes or until juices run clear when loaf is pierced with a knife. Let stand in pan 10 minutes. Makes 4 to 6 servings.

Lamb with Pine Nuts & Raisins

Flavors of the Middle East will make this one of your favorites.

1 pound lean ground lamb
1 small onion, finely chopped
1 garlic clove, minced
1/2 cup pine nuts
1/2 cup raisins
2 cups cooked couscous
1/4 cup brandy or apple juice
1 teaspoon ground cinnamon
1/2 teaspoon ground coriander
Salt and freshly ground pepper

Preheat oven to 350°F (175°C). Grease an 8″ × 4″ loaf pan.

Combine lamb, onion, garlic, pine nuts, raisins, couscous, brandy, cinnamon, coriander, salt, and pepper in a medium-size bowl. Transfer mixture to loaf pan.

Cover with foil and bake 30 minutes. Uncover and bake about 30 minutes or until an instant-read thermometer inserted in center reads 165°F (65°C). Let stand in pan 10 minutes. Makes 4 to 6 servings.

Lamb-stuffed Cabbage Loaf

Remember stuffed cabbage rolls? This is an easier version.

1 pound lean ground lamb
2 cups cooked rice (see Note below)
1 bunch green onions, finely chopped
2 garlic cloves, minced
1/2 cup red wine or apple juice
2 tablespoons soy sauce
1 egg, lightly beaten
1/2 teaspoon dried leaf thyme
Dash of hot pepper sauce
Salt and freshly ground pepper
6 to 8 large cabbage leaves

Preheat oven to 350°F (175°C). Grease a 9″ × 5″ loaf pan. Combine lamb, rice, onions, garlic, wine, soy sauce, egg, thyme, hot pepper sauce, salt, and pepper in a medium-size bowl. Using your hands or an electric mixer, mix until thoroughly combined.

Drop cabbage leaves in boiling water and cook about 2 minutes or until softened. Cool in cold water and remove thick ribs. Use leaves to line loaf pan, letting leaves extend over sides and ends of pan. Carefully spoon lamb mixture into leaves. Bring leaves over lamb mixture and cover pan with foil.

Bake about 1 hour or until juices run clear with pierced with a knife. Let stand 5 minutes, then cut into thick slices. Makes 4 to 6 servings.

Note

One cup uncooked rice yields two to three cups when cooked.

Corned Beef & Potato Loaf

Leftover corned beef works fine for this loaf—a close cousin to corned beef hash.

8 ounces cooked corned beef, coarsely ground
5 small cooked potatoes, mashed but slightly lumpy
1/2 cup finely chopped onion
1/4 cup dry bread crumbs
1 egg, lightly beaten
2 teaspoons Dijon mustard
Freshly ground pepper
1 tablespoon honey

Preheat oven to 350°F (175°C). Grease a 9″ × 5″ nonstick loaf pan. Combine corned beef, potatoes, onion, bread crumbs, egg, 1-1/2 teaspoons of the Dijon mustard, and pepper in a medium-size bowl.

Transfer beef mixture to loaf pan and smooth top.

Bake 40 minutes. Combine remaining 1/2 teaspoon mustard and honey in a small bowl. Brush over top of loaf. Bake 30 minutes or until top is glazed and loaf is set. Makes 4 servings.

Variation

Breakfast Loaf

Make 3 to 4 wells in mixture, each deep enough to hold an egg. Break an egg in a small bowl, then pour into one of the wells. Cover with beef mixture. Repeat with remaining eggs. Omit glaze.

Pork Country Pâté

This is a light, moist pâté that will appeal to most people.

8 ounces chicken livers, rinsed and patted dry
1 pound finely ground lean pork
1 egg, lightly beaten
1 tablespoon dry bread crumbs
1/2 teaspoon ground sage
1/4 teaspoon ground coriander
1 teaspoon salt
Freshly ground pepper
2 bacon slices, diced
1 boneless smoked pork chop, diced
1 small onion, finely chopped
1 garlic clove, minced

Preheat oven to 350°F (175°C). Grease a 9″ × 5″ loaf pan.

Process chicken livers in a food processor until finely ground. Add pork, egg, bread crumbs, sage, coriander, salt, and pepper and process to combine. Transfer mixture to a bowl. Stir in bacon, pork chop, onion, and garlic.

Transfer mixture to loaf pan. Place loaf pan in a baking pan. Add enough hot water to come halfway up sides of loaf pan.

Bake about 1 hour or until top is browned and an instant-read thermometer inserted in center reads 170°F (75°C). Let cool in pan 10 minutes. Drain off any liquid. Makes about 6 servings.

Easy Liver Pâté

Almost no cooking is required to make this easy appetizer.

1 tablespoon olive oil
1/2 cup finely chopped onion
1 garlic clove, minced
2 (8-oz.) packages cream cheese, softened
8 ounces liverwurst, chopped
1/4 cup white wine or apple juice
2 tablespoons chopped flat-leaf parsley
1/4 teaspoon ground sage
Freshly ground pepper

Heat olive oil in a medium-size skillet over medium heat. Add onion and garlic and cook until softened but not brown. Set aside.

Beat cream cheese until light and fluffy. Beat in liverwurst until smooth. Beat in wine, parsley, sage, pepper, and onion mixture. Line a small loaf pan or bowl with plastic wrap. Pack mixture into pan. Cover and refrigerate at least 2 hours or until chilled. This can be made up to a day ahead and refrigerated. Makes about 8 servings.

Ripe Olive Beef Loaf

This tastes like pizza in a loaf—great for hot sandwiches with melted cheese.

1 pound ground beef
1 (8-oz.) can tomato sauce
1/2 cup dry bread crumbs
1/2 cup sliced ripe olives
1/2 cup finely chopped onion
1 garlic clove, minced
1 teaspoon dried leaf basil
Salt and freshly ground pepper

Preheat oven to 350°F (175°C). Grease an 8″ × 4″ loaf pan.

Combine beef, tomato sauce, bread crumbs, olives, onion, garlic, basil, salt, and pepper in a medium-size bowl. Using your hands or an electric mixer, mix until thoroughly combined. Transfer mixture to loaf pan.

Bake 40 minutes or until an instant-read thermometer inserted in center reads 165°F (65°C). Let stand in pan 10 minutes. Makes 4 to 6 servings.

Mexican Bean & Beef Loaf

Serve with a spicy salsa.

1 pound ground beef
1/2 cup chopped onion
1 garlic clove, minced
1 teaspoon chili powder
1/2 teaspoon ground cumin
1/2 teaspoon dried leaf oregano
2 tablespoons beer or water
1 (15-oz.) can refried beans
Salt and freshly ground pepper
2 (10-inch) flour tortillas

Preheat oven to 350°F (175°C). Grease a 9″ × 5″ loaf pan.

Combine beef, onion, garlic, chili powder, cumin, oregano, beer, beans, salt, and pepper in a medium-size bowl.

Line loaf pan with tortillas, overlapping and letting tortillas extend above loaf. Spoon mixture into tortilla-lined loaf pan. Moisten edges of tortillas and fold over meat mixture.

Cover with foil and bake 30 minutes. Uncover and bake about 30 minutes or until an instant-read thermometer inserted in center reads 165°F (65°C). Let stand in pan 10 minutes. Makes 4 servings.

Bell Pepper Loaf

The flavors of stuffed bell peppers are captured in this dense meatloaf.

2 medium-size green bell peppers
1 tablespoon olive oil
1 cup finely chopped onion
1 garlic clove, minced
1 pound lean ground beef
1 pound ground turkey
1 cup cooked white rice (see Note, page 23)
1 egg, lightly beaten
1 teaspoon dried leaf oregano
1 teaspoon salt
Freshly ground pepper
1 (12-oz.) can tomato sauce

Preheat oven to 350°F (175°C). Grease a 9″ × 5″ loaf pan. Roast bell peppers over a flame or under the broiler, turning, until blistered on all sides. Cool in a sealed paper bag and remove skin. Cut into halves, remove cores, and cut off tops and bottoms to make straight, flat pieces.

Heat olive oil in a small skillet over medium heat. Add onion and garlic and cook until softened. Combine beef, turkey, rice, egg, oregano, salt, pepper, and onion mixture in a large bowl. Using your hands or an electric mixer, mix until thoroughly combined.

Pat one-third of meat mixture into loaf pan. Layer half the bell peppers over meat mixture. Pat another third of meat mixture over the bell peppers. Layer remaining bell peppers over meat mixture and top with remaining third of meat mixture.

Bake 45 minutes. Drain off any fat and pour tomato sauce over loaf. Bake 15 minutes or until meat mixture is cooked through and an instant-read thermometer inserted in center reads 170°F (70°C). Let stand in pan 10 minutes before cutting into slices. Makes 6 servings.

Greek-style Meatloaf

Use lean ground lamb for this if it is available;
if not, drain the fat from the loaf after 30 minutes of baking.

1 small eggplant
1 pound ground lamb
1/3 cup chopped ripe Greek olives
1 large plum tomato, finely chopped
1/2 small onion, minced
1 garlic clove, minced
1 teaspoon dried leaf oregano
Salt and freshly ground pepper
1 (13-3/4-oz.) can artichoke hearts, drained and rinsed
2/3 cup crumbled feta cheese

Preheat oven to 350°F (175°C). Place eggplant in a small baking pan. Bake about 1 hour or until eggplant is soft. Set aside to cool. Peel and finely chop eggplant.

Grease a 9″ × 5″ loaf pan. Combine eggplant, lamb, olives, tomato, onion, garlic, oregano, salt, and pepper in a medium-size bowl. Spoon half of lamb mixture into loaf pan. Arrange 2 rows of artichoke hearts down the center of the loaf. Sprinkle with half of the feta cheese. Spoon remaining lamb mixture into pan, pressing down slightly.

Bake 1 hour. Sprinkle top of loaf with remaining feta cheese. Bake until cheese melts and an instant-read thermometer inserted in center of loaf reads 165°F (75°C). Let stand 20 minutes before cutting. Makes 6 servings.

Grilled Cheeseburger Loaf

All the traditional cheeseburger ingredients are inside the loaf. It's perfect for summer because you don't have to heat the oven.

1 pound lean ground beef
1 small onion, finely chopped
1 egg, lightly beaten
2 tablespoons sweet pickle relish
2 tablespoons ketchup
1 tablespoon prepared mustard
Salt and freshly ground pepper
2 ounces shredded Cheddar cheese (1/2 cup)

Preheat grill for indirect cooking. Combine meat, onion, egg, relish, ketchup, mustard, salt, and pepper in a bowl. Using your hands or an electric mixer, mix until thoroughly combined.

Shape into a 7-inch round. Place in a grill basket or directly on the grill rack. Cook in center of grill, away from direct heat.

Cook, turning once, about 30 minutes or until no longer pink in center. Sprinkle top with cheese and cook until cheese melts.

Cut into wedges to serve. Makes 3 or 4 servings.

Blue Cheese Meatloaf

The cheese melts but the flavor remains.

1 pound ground beef
1/4 pound ground pork
1 egg, lightly beaten
1/2 cup fresh bread crumbs
1/2 cup finely chopped onion
1 garlic clove, minced
1 tablespoon chopped fresh flat-leaf parsley
1 tablespoon Worcestershire sauce
Freshly ground pepper
2 ounces crumbled blue cheese

Preheat oven to 375°F (190°C). Grease an 8″ × 4″ loaf pan. Combine beef, pork, egg, bread crumbs, onion, garlic, parsley, Worcestershire sauce, and pepper in a medium-size bowl. Stir in blue cheese.

Transfer meat mixture to loaf pan. Bake 50 minutes or until an instant-read thermometer inserted in center of loaf registers 165°F (75°C). Drain off fat. Let stand 10 minutes before cutting. Makes 3 or 4 servings.

Old-Fashioned Meatloaf

The standard proportion for meatloaf is two parts beef to one part pork. In fact, many supermarkets sell ground beef and pork packaged this way. The fat in the pork makes a juicy loaf.

1 pound ground beef
1/2 pound ground pork
1 small onion, minced
1 small green bell pepper, finely chopped
1 cup fresh bread crumbs
1/2 cup ketchup or tomato sauce
1 egg, lightly beaten
1-1/2 teaspoons salt
Freshly ground pepper

Preheat oven to 350°F (175°C). Spray a 9″ × 5″ loaf pan with nonstick cooking spray or lightly grease.

Combine beef, pork, onion, bell pepper, bread crumbs, ketchup, egg, salt, and pepper in a medium-size bowl. Using your hands or an electric mixer, mix until thoroughly combined.

Transfer meat mixture to loaf pan. Bake about 1 hour and 15 minutes or until loaf is browned. Let stand 10 minutes, then cut loaf into thick slices. Makes 4 to 6 servings.

Lowbush Moose (Rabbit) Loaf

Rabbit or hare, often the wild variety, is eaten frequently in Alaska, where it's often called "lowbush moose." Fortunately for us, rabbit is often available frozen in the meat section of the supermarket or can be special-ordered.

1 (about 2-1/2 lb.) rabbit, cut into serving pieces
1 carrot
1 celery stalk with leaves
1 bay leaf
1 large onion slice
1 teaspoon peppercorns
1/2 cup minced onion
2 tablespoons finely chopped flat-leaf parsley
1 cup cracker crumbs
1/2 cup shredded Swiss cheese (2 ounces)
1/2 cup light sour cream
1/2 cup white wine or apple juice
1 egg, lightly beaten
1/2 teaspoon rubbed sage
Salt and freshly ground pepper

Rinse rabbit. Place rabbit, carrot, celery, bay leaf, onion slice, and peppercorns in a Dutch oven. Add enough water to cover. Bring to a boil, reduce heat, cover, and simmer about 1 hour or until rabbit is tender enough to come off bone easily. Remove rabbit from broth. Strain broth, discard vegetables, and refrigerate for another use. Cool and remove rabbit meat from bones.

Preheat oven to 350°F (175°C). Grease a 9″ × 5″ loaf pan. Coarsely chop rabbit meat in a food processor in two batches. Combine minced onion, parsley, crumbs, cheese, sour cream, wine, egg, sage, salt, and pepper in a large bowl. Add rabbit and stir to combine. Transfer to loaf pan and smooth top.

Bake about 45 minutes or until loaf is browned. Makes about 4 servings.

Note

Rabbit is easily removed from the bone after cooking.

Buffalo Loaf

*Buffalo meat is lean and low in cholesterol. Buffaloes are now raised on ranches
and the meat is available as roasts, steaks, and ground meat.*

2 pounds ground buffalo
1 cup minced onion
1/2 cup minced celery
1 garlic clove, minced
1/2 cup fresh bread crumbs
1/2 cup tomato juice
1 egg, lightly beaten
1 tablespoon Worcestershire sauce
Salt and freshly ground pepper

Preheat oven to 350°F (175°C). Spray a 13″ × 9″ baking pan with nonstick cooking spray or lightly grease.

Combine meat, onion, celery, garlic, bread crumbs, tomato juice, egg, Worcestershire sauce, salt, and pepper in a medium-size bowl. Using your hands or an electric mixer, mix until thoroughly combined.

Shape meat mixture into an oval loaf in pan. Bake about 1 hour and 15 minutes or until loaf is browned. Let stand 10 minutes, then cut into thick slices. Makes 6 to 8 servings.

Ham & Potato Salad Loaf

The layers of bright green, pink, and creamy white make an attractive loaf that is perfect for picnics—just take it in a cooler still in the loaf pan.

Potato Salad (see below)
Ham Salad (see below)
1 (10-oz.) package fresh spinach, rinsed

Potato Salad:

3 cups mashed potatoes
1/2 cup finely chopped celery
1 tablespoon seasoned rice vinegar
1 tablespoon olive oil
1/4 cup lowfat plain yogurt
1/4 cup mayonnaise
2 tablespoons chopped parsley
1/2 teaspoon dried dill weed
Salt and freshly ground pepper to taste

Ham Salad:

1 pound finely chopped ham
2 tablespoons finely chopped sweet pickles
1/2 cup mayonnaise
1/4 cup low-fat plain yogurt
1 tablespoon Dijon mustard

Prepare salads and set aside. Blanch spinach in boiling water until limp but still bright green. Drain and immediately place in ice water to stop the cooking. Drain spinach and pat dry with paper towels. Carefully cut off large stems.

Line a 9″ × 5″ loaf pan with plastic wrap, letting ends extend over edges of pan. Line bottom and sides of pan with spinach leaves, letting some leaves extend over edges of pan.

Spoon half the Potato Salad into bottom of spinach-lined pan, packing firmly. Top with Ham Salad, then remaining Potato Salad. Arrange a row of spinach leaves over top of loaf, then bring over leaves from edges to completely cover top. Bring edges of plastic wrap over loaf to cover. Refrigerate at least 4 hours or overnight. To serve, uncover top and turn out loaf on a platter. Cut into thick slices with a serrated knife. Makes about 4 servings.

Potato Salad

Combine potatoes, celery, rice vinegar, and oil in a large bowl. Combine yogurt, mayonnaise, parsley, dill, salt, and pepper in a small bowl. Stir yogurt mixture into potato mixture until blended.

Ham Salad

Combine ham, pickles, mayonnaise, yogurt, and mustard in a large bowl.

Ham & Sweet Potato Loaf

Serve with steamed Brussels sprouts and Mashed Potatoes (page 114).

1 pound lean ground pork
1/2 pound ground ham
2 cups mashed cooked sweet potatoes
1 egg, lightly beaten
1/4 cup bourbon or apple juice
1/4 teaspoon dried leaf thyme
1/2 teaspoon salt
Freshly ground pepper

Preheat oven to 350°F (175°C). Grease a 9″ × 5″ loaf pan. Combine pork, ham, sweet potatoes, egg, bourbon, thyme, salt, and pepper in a medium-size bowl. Using your hands or an electric mixer, mix until thoroughly combined. Transfer mixture to loaf pan.

Bake about 70 minutes or until loaf is browned and firm. Let stand 10 minutes. Drain off any liquid. Makes 4 to 6 servings.

Ham & Arugula Loaf

I'm delighted that arugula is more widely available and I no longer have to grow my own. Its slightly bitter flavor goes well with this mixture.

1 pound ground ham
1 tablespoon dry bread crumbs
1 egg, lightly beaten
1 ounce arugula, finely chopped
1/4 teaspoon dried leaf thyme
1/4 teaspoon dried leaf oregano
Freshly ground pepper
1/2 (17-1/2-oz.) package frozen puff pastry, thawed
3 ounces Swiss cheese slices
1 egg white, lightly beaten
1 tablespoon sesame seeds

Preheat oven to 350°F (175°C). Grease a baking sheet. Combine ham, bread crumbs, egg, arugula, thyme, oregano, and pepper in a medium-size bowl.

Roll out pastry on a lightly floured board into a 14″ × 11″ rectangle. Place one-half of ham mixture in center third of pastry, leaving about 2 inches on each end. Shape ham mixture into a loaf. Top with cheese. Pat remaining ham mixture over cheese, keeping the loaf shape. Bring up pastry and seal edges. Place loaf seam side down on baking sheet.

Brush pastry with egg white and sprinkle with sesame seeds. Bake about 50 minutes or until pastry is golden brown. Let stand 10 minutes before removing from pan. Cut into thick slices to serve. Makes 4 servings.

Mediterranean Breakfast Loaves

*To serve this as part of a picnic breakfast, leave loaves wrapped in foil, then wrap
in several layers of newspapers, sealing with tape. Loaf will stay warm
at least 1 hour. Add a container of juice and one of
hot café au lait. Good eating.*

---

4 (4- or 5-inch) round French bread loaves
1 (14-oz.) can artichoke hearts, drained and rinsed
5 eggs, lightly beaten
2 tablespoons milk
1 tablespoon chopped fresh basil or 1 teaspoon dried leaf basil
2 teaspoons chopped fresh oregano or 3/4 teaspoon dried leaf oregano
Salt and freshly ground pepper
2 tablespoons butter or margarine
6 ounces fresh mushrooms, sliced
4 ounces thinly sliced cooked ham
4 ounces Brie cheese, cut into thin slices
1 small roasted red bell pepper, cut into strips
1/2 cup shredded Monterey Jack cheese (2 ounces)
1 medium-size tomato, diced

Preheat oven to 350°F (175°C). Cut a thin slice off top of each loaf; set aside. Remove soft interior of each loaf with a fork, leaving a 1-inch-thick wall.

Cut artichoke hearts into halves. Process in a food processor until coarsely chopped; set aside. Beat eggs, milk, basil, oregano, salt, and pepper in a medium-size bowl. Stir in chopped artichoke hearts. Set aside.

Melt butter in a large nonstick skillet over medium heat. Add mushrooms and sauté until mushrooms are limp and liquid evaporates. Spoon mushrooms into a bowl.

Add egg mixture to skillet and cook, stirring occasionally, until soft scrambled.

Place one-fourth of the ham in bottom of each loaf. Top with one-eighth of the mushrooms, then 1 slice Brie cheese. Spoon one-fourth of the scrambled eggs over cheese in each loaf. Arrange one-fourth of the bell pepper over eggs. Top with remaining mushrooms and Monterey Jack cheese. Finally divide tomato equally among loaves and replace tops of loaves.

Wrap each loaf in foil and place on a baking sheet. Bake 20 minutes or until interior is hot and cheese melts. Makes 4 servings.

Ham & Apple Loaf

Apples complement the smoky ham flavor.

1 pound ground ham
1/2 small onion, minced
1/2 small apple, finely chopped
2 tablespoons dry bread crumbs
1/4 teaspoon dried leaf thyme
1 egg, lightly beaten
1 teaspoon Dijon mustard
Freshly ground pepper

Preheat oven to 350°F (175°C). Grease a 13″ × 9″ baking pan. Combine all ingredients in a medium-size bowl. Shape mixture into a round loaf, about 8 inches in diameter, in pan.

Bake 40 minutes or until top is browned and loaf is set. Let stand 10 minutes before removing from pan. Cut into wedges to serve. Makes 4 servings.

Variation

To cut the saltiness of the ham, add one-half pound ground pork to the recipe and use the whole apple.

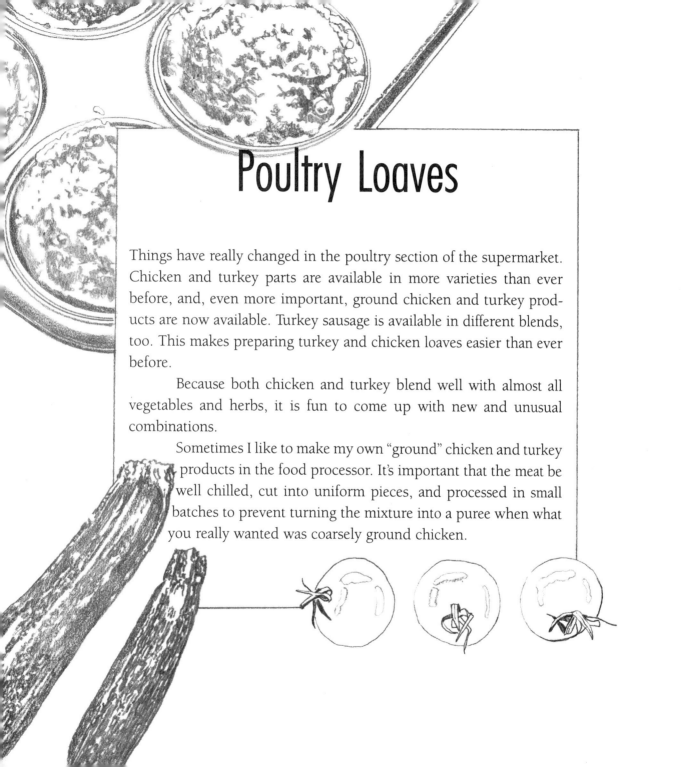

Poultry Loaves

Things have really changed in the poultry section of the supermarket. Chicken and turkey parts are available in more varieties than ever before, and, even more important, ground chicken and turkey products are now available. Turkey sausage is available in different blends, too. This makes preparing turkey and chicken loaves easier than ever before.

Because both chicken and turkey blend well with almost all vegetables and herbs, it is fun to come up with new and unusual combinations.

Sometimes I like to make my own "ground" chicken and turkey products in the food processor. It's important that the meat be well chilled, cut into uniform pieces, and processed in small batches to prevent turning the mixture into a puree when what you really wanted was coarsely ground chicken.

Chicken & Mushroom Loaf

The mushrooms and aromatic vegetables add just the right flavors to this tasty firm loaf that forms perfect slices.

1 tablespoon olive oil
4 ounces fresh mushrooms, finely chopped
1 large celery stalk, finely chopped
1 medium-size onion, finely chopped
1 small carrot, finely shredded
1 pound ground chicken
1 cup fresh bread crumbs
1 egg, lightly beaten
1 teaspoon dried leaf basil
1 teaspoon rosemary
Salt and freshly ground pepper

Preheat oven to 350°F (175°C). Grease an 8″ × 4″ loaf pan. Heat olive oil in a large skillet over medium heat. Add mushrooms, celery, onion, and carrot. Cook until vegetables are softened and liquid disappears. Let cool.

Add chicken, bread crumbs, egg, basil, rosemary, salt, and pepper to vegetables. Transfer to loaf pan.

Bake about 1 hour or until golden brown. Let stand in pan 10 minutes. Serve warm. Makes 4 servings.

Double Turkey, Ham & Cheese Roll

Serve this elegant roll with Fresh Tomato Sauce (page 117).

About 1 pound turkey cutlets
1 pound lean ground turkey
1/4 cup Italian bread crumbs
1 egg, lightly beaten
1/4 cup minced green onions
1 garlic clove, minced
1 cup shredded Swiss cheese (4 ounces)
4 ounces sliced cooked ham

Preheat oven to 375°F (190°C). Grease a jellyroll pan. Place turkey cutlets between layers of plastic wrap. Pound out to 1/4-inch thickness. Arrange cutlets on waxed paper in about a 13″ × 9″ rectangle.

Combine ground turkey, bread crumbs, egg, green onions, and garlic in a medium-size bowl. Sprinkle 1/4 of the cheese over turkey cutlets. Arrange ham in a row down center of rectangle. Pat ground turkey mixture in an even layer over rectangle. Sprinkle with remaining cheese.

Roll up jellyroll style, starting at one long side and using waxed paper to aid in rolling. Place seam side down in pan.

Bake about 45 minutes or until loaf is browned and an instant-read thermometer inserted in center reads 170°F (75°C). Let stand 10 minutes before slicing. Makes about 6 servings.

Caribbean Chicken Loaf

*In Jamaica, they would probably add the scorching hot Scotch Bonnet chiles,
but I prefer the* pasilla *chile that has more flavor and just a touch of heat.
Serve with black beans and yellow rice.*

1 large very ripe plantain
1 pound ground chicken
4 finely chopped corn tortillas (about 1/2 cup)
1 pasilla chile, finely chopped
1/2 red bell pepper, finely chopped
1/4 cup finely chopped onion
1/2 cup fresh lime juice
1 egg, lightly beaten
Salt and freshly ground black pepper

Preheat oven to 350°F (175°C). Wrap plantain in foil. Bake about 1 hour or until very soft. Cool, peel, and mash.

Grease a 9″ × 5″ loaf pan. Combine plantain, chicken, tortillas, chile, bell pepper, onion, lime juice, egg, salt, and black pepper in a large bowl. Transfer chicken mixture to loaf pan.

Bake 1 hour or until loaf is browned and an instant-read thermometer inserted in center reads 170°F (75°C). Let stand in pan 10 minutes. Makes 4 to 6 servings.

Duck Loaf

Serve in thin slices with a hearty whole-grain bread, fruit chutney, and cornichons.

1 (4-1/2-lb.) duck
1/2 cup red wine
1 garlic clove, minced
1 teaspoon grated gingerroot
8 ounces chicken livers, rinsed
8 ounces bulk turkey sausage
1 egg, lightly beaten
2 tablespoons dry bread crumbs
1 teaspoon salt
1/4 teaspoon ground coriander
1 tablespoon green peppercorns, drained
1 small onion, finely chopped

Rinse duck. Cut down back of duck with kitchen shears or a knife. Remove carcass from duck, being careful not to make holes in skin. Cut all meat from skin and set aside. Remove some fat from skin and refrigerate skin until needed. Cut meat from breast and legs. Cut meat into about 1-inch pieces and place in a bowl. Add wine, garlic, and gingerroot. Cover and refrigerate at least 1 hour.

Preheat oven to 375°F (190°C). Arrange duck skin, fat side up, in the top part of a loaf pan set with holes to drain off fat, draping excess skin over sides of pan.

Drain duck, discarding wine. Process chicken liver until pureed. Add sausage, egg, bread crumbs, salt, and coriander. Process just to combine. Stir in peppercorns, onion, and marinated duck. Spoon mixture into skin. Bring sides of skin over filling. Trim off excess skin with kitchen shears. Add 1 inch water to bottom pan. Place top pan in place.

Bake about 1 hour or until juices run clear when loaf is pierced in center. (Remove from oven and drain fat from bottom pan if needed during baking.) Skin will shrink from top of loaf as it bakes. Remove top pan and cool slightly on a rack. Wrap in foil, place another loaf pan with canned vegetables in pan for a weight, and refrigerate overnight. Remove from pan and remove skin from loaf. Makes about 8 servings.

Chicken Cordon Bleu Loaf

This is my husband's favorite loaf. It's also delicious cold, if there's any left.

3 boneless, skinless chicken breast halves
4 tablespoons Italian bread crumbs
6 ounces cooked ham slices
6 ounces provolone cheese slices

Preheat oven to 375°F (190°C). Grease an 8″ × 4″ loaf pan. Place chicken breasts between layers of plastic wrap. Pound out each half to a rectangle about 8″ × 4″.

Place 1 chicken breast in bottom of loaf pan. Sprinkle with 1 tablespoon bread crumbs. Top crumbs with a layer of cheese, then a layer of ham. Repeat layers, ending with a layer of crumbs.

Bake about 1 hour or until chicken is cooked through. Let stand in pan 15 minutes. Cut into 4 slices to serve. Makes 4 servings.

Variation

Turkey cutlets can be substituted for the chicken.

Layered Turkey, Cheese & Spinach Terrine

The spinach mixture is the key to this loaf, which combines most of my favorite flavors.

1 (10-oz.) package frozen chopped spinach, thawed and squeezed dry or 1 (10-oz.) package fresh
   spinach, cooked, squeezed dry, and chopped
4 ounces feta cheese, finely crumbled
1 tablespoon sun-dried tomato paste
1 large garlic clove, minced
2 teaspoons dried leaf basil
Freshly ground black pepper
1/2 (17-1/2-oz.) package frozen puff pastry, thawed
8 ounces mesquite-smoked cooked turkey, thinly sliced
4 to 6 ounces provolone cheese, thinly sliced
1 (7-oz.) jar roasted red bell peppers, drained and cut into strips
Milk

Preheat oven to 375°F (190°C). Grease an 8″ × 4″ loaf pan. Process spinach, feta cheese, tomato paste, garlic, basil, and pepper in a food processor until combined.

Roll out pastry on a lightly floured board into a 14″ × 11″ rectangle. Fit pastry into loaf pan, letting pastry extend over sides and ends.

Layer turkey, spinach mixture, provolone cheese, and roasted peppers in that order in loaf, making three layers of each. Bring pastry over filling. Brush with milk and seal edges. Cut vents to allow steam to escape.

Bake about 45 minutes or until pastry is golden brown. Cool in pan on a rack 10 minutes, then remove from pan and cool on a rack 5 minutes before cutting. Serve warm. Makes about 6 servings.

 Note

Sun-dried tomato paste is available in a tube. Regular tomato paste can be substituted.

Chicken & Zucchini Crepe Loaf

If you like crepes, you will love this loaf that's perfect for lunch or brunch.

Crepe batter (see below)
1 pound ground chicken
1/4 cup finely chopped onion
1 garlic clove, minced
2 zucchini, shredded (2 cups)
1 carrot, shredded
2 tablespoons all-purpose flour
3/4 cup milk
1/4 cup sherry
1/2 teaspoon dried leaf tarragon
Salt and freshly ground pepper
1 cup shredded Swiss cheese (4 ounces)

Crepe Batter:
3/4 cup all-purpose flour
1/2 teaspoon salt
1 cup milk
3 eggs
2 tablespoons vegetable oil

Prepare batter for crepes. Spray a 16″ × 10″ nonstick griddle and place over medium heat. Pour batter quickly over griddle, tilting griddle to spread batter in a thin layer. Cook until golden brown on bottom. Carefully turn crepe; cook until browned on bottom. Invert crepe onto a strip of waxed paper and cool. Cut crepe crosswise into 4 (4-inch) strips.

Preheat oven to 375°F (190°C). Grease an 8″ × 4″ loaf pan. Line bottom and ends of pan with foil, extending foil over ends, and grease foil. Cook chicken, onion, and garlic in a large skillet over medium heat until browned, stirring to break up meat. Add zucchini and carrot and cook, stirring occasionally, until vegetables are softened and moisture evaporates. Sprinkle mixture with flour and stir to combine. Stir in milk and sherry and cook, stirring, until thickened. Add tarragon, salt, and pepper.

To assemble, place 1 crepe in bottom of loaf pan; top with one-third of chicken mixture, then 1/4 cup cheese. Repeat with remaining crepes, reserving final 1/4 cup cheese to add later.

Bake about 30 minutes or until heated through. Sprinkle with remaining cheese. Bake until cheese melts. Let stand in pan 5 minutes. Using the ends of the foil, remove to a plate. Makes 4 servings.

Crepe Batter

Combine flour, salt, milk, eggs, and oil in a blender container. Blend 1 minute; scrape down side of blender. Blend 30 seconds. Refrigerate 1 hour. Blend again briefly before cooking.

Variation

Making one large crepe requires some practice. You can make the crepes as 6 (7-inch) rounds the regular way and just fold over edges to fit the loaf pan.

Italian Turkey Loaf

Turkey and turkey sausage are combined in this loaf with the flavors of Italy.

1 pound ground turkey
1 pound Italian turkey sausage, casings removed
1/2 cup tomato sauce
1/2 cup Italian bread crumbs
1 cup finely chopped fresh mushrooms
1/2 cup shredded mozzarella cheese (2 ounces)
1 teaspoon dried leaf basil
Salt and freshly ground pepper

Preheat oven to 350°F (175°C). Grease a 9″ × 5″ loaf pan. Combine turkey, sausage, tomato sauce, bread crumbs, mushrooms, cheese, basil, salt, and pepper in a medium-size bowl. Transfer mixture to loaf pan.

Bake about 1-1/2 hours or until an instant-read thermometer inserted in center of loaf reads 170°F (75°C). Let stand in pan 10 minutes before cutting. Makes 6 to 8 servings.

Easy Sausage Loaf

Serve as a main dish for brunch or cut into thin slices and serve as an appetizer.
This is best soon after baking.

Dough (see below)
1 pound bulk spicy turkey sausage
All-purpose flour

Dough:

1 (1/4-oz.) package active dry yeast
2 teaspoons sugar
1/4 cup lukewarm water
1/2 cup milk
2 tablespoons butter or margarine, softened
2 cups all-purpose flour
1 teaspoon dry mustard
1 teaspoon salt
Freshly ground pepper
2 tablespoons minced flat-leaf parsley
2 tablespoons minced green onion tops

Prepare dough. Preheat oven to 375°F (190°C). Grease an 8″ × 4″ loaf pan.

Carefully remove sausage from wrapping, leaving sausage whole. Place sausage on a rack in a baking pan. Bake about 45 minutes or until sausage is cooked through. Cool slightly. Lightly coat sausage with flour.

Roll out dough into a 10″ × 8″ rectangle. Place sausage in center of dough with sausage parallel to the short edge. Bring ends of dough over sausage. Overlap sides of dough and brush with water to seal. (Bottom of loaf should be a double thickness of dough.) Place dough-wrapped sausage seam side down in loaf pan. Cut vents in the top to allow steam to escape. Cover loaf and let rise in a warm place about 20 minutes. Preheat oven to 375°F (190°C).

Bake about 30 minutes or until top is golden brown. If sides are not browned, remove from pan and place directly on the oven rack to finish browning. Makes about 6 servings.

Dough

Dissolve yeast and sugar in water in the bowl of an electric mixer. Let stand until foamy, about 5 minutes. Add milk, butter, 1 cup of the flour, mustard, salt, and several grinds of pepper and beat until smooth. Add enough remaining flour to make a soft dough. Knead with the dough hook about 10 minutes or until smooth. Knead in parsley and green onion tops. Cover bowl and let rise in a warm place until doubled in bulk, about 45 minutes. Punch down dough and shape into a ball.

Notes

After the first rising, the dough can be placed in a greased bowl, covered, and refrigerated overnight. If dough is cold, it will take longer to rise after shaping the loaf. The sausage can also be cooked ahead and refrigerated overnight.

Flouring the sausage helps the dough stick to it during baking and prevents the dough from pulling away and leaving a large gap between it and the sausage.

Artichoke-Chicken Loaf

The chicken is finely ground in a food processor. With its delicate flavor, the loaf is good hot or cold.

3 tablespoons butter or margarine
1 cup chopped onion
1 (14-oz.) can artichoke hearts, drained and rinsed
1 pound boneless skinless chicken, dark and white meat combined
1/4 cup dry bread crumbs
1 egg
1/4 cup half-and-half
1 teaspoon dried leaf tarragon
1 teaspoon salt
Freshly ground pepper

Preheat oven to 350°F (175°C). Grease an 8″ × 4″ loaf pan. Melt butter in a medium-size skillet over medium heat. Add onion and cook until softened. Let cool.

Process artichoke hearts in a food processor until finely chopped; turn into a bowl. Cut chicken into 1-inch pieces. Add chicken to food processor in two batches. Process until coarsely chopped, scraping down bowl frequently. Add onion, bread crumbs, egg, half-and-half, tarragon, salt, and pepper to chicken. Process until finely chopped. Add artichokes and process just to combine.

Transfer mixture to loaf pan. Place loaf pan in a baking pan. Add enough hot water to come halfway up sides of loaf pan.

Bake about 1 hour or until top is browned and an instant-read thermometer inserted in center reads 170°F (75°C). Let cool in pan 10 minutes. Drain off any liquid and turn out loaf onto a plate. Makes about 4 servings.

Touch-of-the-Orient Chicken Loaf

Delicious served hot with a mustard sauce, or cover and refrigerate overnight.
Cut into small cubes and serve with a mustardy dipping sauce.

3 tablespoons butter or margarine
1 cup chopped onion
2 garlic cloves, minced
1 pound boneless, skinless chicken, dark and white meat combined
1 egg
1/4 cup dry bread crumbs
1/4 cup hoisin sauce
1 (8-oz.) can sliced water chestnuts, drained
1 teaspoon five-spice powder
1 teaspoon grated gingerroot
1/2 teaspoon salt
Freshly ground pepper

Preheat oven to 350°F (175°C). Grease an 8″ × 4″ loaf pan. Melt butter in a medium-size skillet over medium heat. Add onion and garlic and cook until softened. Let cool.

Cut chicken into 1-inch pieces. Add chicken, egg, bread crumbs, and hoisin sauce to a food processor. Process until coarsely chopped, scraping down bowl frequently. Add onion mixture, water chestnuts, five-spice powder, gingerroot, salt, and pepper. Process until finely chopped.

Spoon mixture into prepared pan. Place loaf pan in a baking pan. Add enough hot water to come halfway up sides of loaf pan.

Bake about 1 hour or until top is browned and an instant-read thermometer inserted in center reads 170°F (75°C). Let cool in pan 10 minutes. Drain off any liquid and turn out loaf onto a plate. Makes 4 servings.

Curried Chicken Loaf

The surprise ingredient here is canned peaches.

2 tablespoons olive oil
1/2 cup chopped onion
1 garlic clove, minced
1 pound boneless skinless chicken, dark and white meat combined
1 egg
1 (8-oz.) can peaches, well drained
3/4 cup fresh bread crumbs
2 teaspoons curry powder
1/2 teaspoon ground cinnamon
1 teaspoon salt
Freshly ground pepper

Preheat oven to 350°F (175°C). Grease an 8″ × 4″ loaf pan. Heat oil in a medium-size skillet over medium heat. Add onion and garlic and cook until softened. Let cool.

Cut chicken into 1-inch pieces. Add chicken, egg, and peaches to a food processor. Process until coarsely chopped, scraping down bowl frequently. Add onion mixture, bread crumbs, curry powder, cinnamon, salt, and pepper. Process until finely chopped.

Transfer mixture to loaf pan. Place loaf pan in a baking pan. Add enough water to come halfway up sides of loaf pan.

Bake about 1 hour or until juices run clear when loaf is pierced in center. Let cool 10 minutes. Drain off any liquid and turn out loaf onto a plate. Makes 3 or 4 servings.

Southwest Bean–Chicken Loaf

The blue corn chips add random layers of color to this firm loaf made with beans and chicken.
Serve with tomatillo salsa.

3 tablespoons butter or margarine
1 cup chopped onion
2 garlic cloves, minced
1 (15-oz.) can Great Northern beans, drained and rinsed
1 pound boneless skinless chicken, dark and white meat combined
1 egg
1/4 cup white wine or apple juice
1 cup diced plum tomatoes
2 cups crumbled blue tortilla chips
1 teaspoon ground cumin
1/2 teaspoon ground coriander
1 teaspoon salt
Freshly ground pepper

Preheat oven to 350°F (175°C). Grease an 8″ × 4″ loaf pan. Melt butter in a medium-size skillet over medium heat. Add onion and garlic and cook until softened. Let cool.

Process beans in a food processor until finely chopped; turn into a bowl. Cut chicken into 1-inch pieces. Add chicken to food processor in two batches. Process until coarsely chopped, scraping down bowl frequently. Add onion mixture, egg, and wine. Process until finely chopped. Add to beans, with tomatoes, tortilla chips, cumin, coriander, salt, and pepper and stir to combine.

Transfer mixture to loaf pan. Place loaf pan in a baking pan. Add enough hot water to come halfway up sides of loaf pan.

Bake about 1 hour or until top is browned and an instant-read thermometer inserted in center reads 170°F (75°C). Let cool 10 minutes. Turn out loaf onto a plate. Makes 4 to 6 servings.

Chicken & Vegetable Loaf

The chicken is left coarser here—more like the texture of a country pâté.

3 tablespoons butter or margarine
1 cup chopped onion
2 garlic cloves, minced
1 pound boneless skinless chicken, dark and white meat combined
1 egg
2 tablespoons fresh lemon juice
1 teaspoon dried rosemary
1 teaspoon salt
Freshly ground pepper
1/4 cup finely chopped sun-dried tomatoes
1 large carrot, diced
1 cup frozen green peas, thawed

Preheat oven to 350°F (175°C). Grease an 8″ × 4″ loaf pan. Melt butter in a medium-size skillet over medium heat. Add onion and garlic and cook until softened. Let cool.

Cut chicken into 1-inch pieces. Add chicken to a food processor. Process until coarsely chopped, scraping down bowl frequently. Add onion mixture, egg, lemon juice, rosemary, salt, and pepper. Process until combined.

Turn out chicken mixture into a medium-size bowl. Stir in tomatoes, carrot, and peas. Transfer mixture to loaf pan. Place loaf pan in a baking pan. Add enough water to come halfway up sides of loaf pan.

Bake about 1 hour or until juices run clear when loaf is pierced in center. Let cool 10 minutes. Drain off any liquid and turn out loaf onto a plate. Cover and refrigerate to serve cold or serve warm. Makes 4 servings.

Variation

Refrigerate wrapped loaf overnight. Roll out 1 sheet thawed frozen puff pastry into a 14″ × 11″ rectangle. Fit over loaf, seal seams, and brush with milk. Bake on a baking sheet in a preheated 400°F (205°C) oven until golden brown, about 30 minutes.

Spinach & Basil–Stuffed Turkey Loaf with Easy Tomato Sauce

Easy and elegant, this loaf has Italian flavors. Serve with Easy Tomato Sauce (page 118).

Spinach-Basil Stuffing (see below)
2 pounds ground turkey
1/3 cup Italian dry bread crumbs
1 egg, lightly beaten
1 cup milk
1 teaspoon salt
1/2 teaspoon dried leaf oregano
Freshly ground pepper
Easy Tomato Sauce (page 118)

Spinach-Basil Stuffing:

1 (10-oz.) package fresh spinach, cooked or 1 (10-oz.) package frozen spinach, thawed
1/2 cup fresh basil
1 garlic clove, minced
1 cup shredded mozzarella cheese (4 ounces)
Salt and freshly ground pepper

Preheat oven to 350°F (175°C). Grease a baking pan. Prepare stuffing. Combine turkey, bread crumbs, egg, milk, salt, oregano, and pepper in a medium-size bowl.

Pat out turkey mixture into a 10″ × 8″ rectangle on a piece of waxed paper. Spread stuffing over turkey mixture. Beginning with one long side, roll up jellyroll style. Using waxed paper, transfer roll to baking pan.

Bake about 1 hour or until an instant-read thermometer inserted in center of loaf registers 170°F (75°C). Let stand 10 minutes before slicing. Makes 6 servings.

Spinach-Basil Stuffing:

Press most of the moisture from spinach. Process spinach, basil, and garlic in a food processor until finely chopped. Add cheese, salt, and pepper; process just to combine.

Variation

Add 1/2 cup toasted pine nuts to spinach stuffing.

Southwestern Chile–Turkey Loaf with Guacamole

The creamy guacamole adds just the right touch to this loaf, made from Southwestern flavors.

1 pound ground turkey
1 cup shredded Monterey Jack cheese (4 ounces)
1/2 cup fresh bread crumbs
4 mild green chiles, roasted, peeled, and chopped or 1 (4-oz.) can chopped green chiles, drained
1 egg, lightly beaten
3 tablespoons salsa
1/4 teaspoon dried leaf oregano
1/4 teaspoon ground cumin
Salt and freshly ground pepper

Guacamole:

1 ripe avocado
1 small tomato, finely chopped
1 tablespoon chopped cilantro
2 tablespoons lemon juice

Preheat oven to 375°F (190°C). Grease an 8″ × 4″ loaf pan. Combine turkey, cheese, bread crumbs, chiles, egg, salsa, oregano, cumin, salt, and pepper in a medium-size bowl. Transfer turkey mixture to loaf pan.

Bake about 1 hour or until an instant-read thermometer inserted in center of loaf reads 170°F (75°C). Let stand in pan 10 minutes. Prepare Guacamole. Turn out loaf on a serving plate and serve with Guacamole on the side. Makes 4 servings.

Guacamole

Mash avocado in a small bowl. Stir in remaining ingredients.

Turkey-stuffed Masa Cups

Masa harina is used to prepare corn tortillas.

1-1/2 cups (about 13 oz.) prepared masa
1 pound ground turkey
1/2 cup minced onion
1 garlic clove, minced
1/2 teaspoon hot pepper sauce
1/2 teaspoon dried leaf oregano
Salt and freshly ground pepper

Preheat oven to 350°F (175°C). Spray 6 large nonstick muffin cups with nonstick cooking spray. Press 1/4 cup masa into bottom and two-thirds up sides of muffin cups.

Using your hands or an electric mixer, combine turkey, onion, garlic, hot pepper sauce, oregano, salt, and pepper in a large bowl.

Fill each masa cup with about 1/3 cup of turkey mixture. Bake 45 minutes or until cooked through. Turn out to serve. Serve with Mango-Tomatillo Salsa (page 119). Makes 6 servings.

Variations

If prepared masa is not available, masa mix is available in the baking section of the supermarket. Follow package directions.

Or you can use a standard pie crust recipe to make the crust.

Spicy Polenta Sausage Loaf

This loaf is best served warm, not hot. Leftovers will be very firm and can be cut into thick slices and fried in olive oil.

Polenta (see below)
1 tablespoon olive oil
3 Italian turkey sausages, cut into 1-inch pieces
1 medium-size onion, chopped
2 garlic cloves, minced
1 medium-size Portbello mushroom (about 2 ounces)
3 plum tomatoes, coarsely chopped
2 teaspoons dried leaf basil
1 teaspoon dried leaf oregano
1/2 teaspoon hot chile flakes or to taste
1 egg, lightly beaten
1 cup shredded Monterey Jack cheese (4 ounces)

Polenta:

1-1/2 cups cornmeal
2-1/2 cups water
2 cups chicken broth
1 teaspoon salt
Freshly ground pepper

Preheat oven to 375°F (190°C). Grease a 9″ × 5″ loaf pan. Prepare Polenta.

Heat olive oil in a large skillet over medium heat. Add sausages, onion, garlic, and mushroom. Cook, stirring occasionally, until sausages are browned. Stir in tomatoes, basil, oregano, and chile flakes. Let cool.

Stir sausage mixture, egg, and cheese into Polenta. Transfer mixture to loaf pan.

Bake about 1 hour or until loaf is browned. Let stand 20 minutes. Loaf will be soft. Makes 6 servings.

Polenta

Mix cornmeal and water together in a medium-size bowl. Bring broth to a boil. Stir cornmeal mixture into broth and cook, stirring, over medium heat until mixture is very thick, about 10 minutes. Add salt and pepper.

Turkey-Applesauce Loaf

The applesauce adds flavor and moisture and prevents the loaf from being dry. This healthy loaf is easy to make and will get compliments from family and friends.

2 pounds ground turkey
1 cup applesauce
1/2 cup dry bread crumbs
1 egg, lightly beaten
1 tablespoon capers, finely chopped
1 teaspoon dried leaf thyme
Salt and freshly ground pepper

Preheat oven to 350°F (175°C). Grease a baking sheet. Combine turkey, applesauce, bread crumbs, egg, capers, thyme, salt, and pepper in a medium-size bowl.

Pat out turkey mixture into a 9″ × 6″ rectangle on baking sheet.

Bake about 1 hour and 15 minutes or until top is browned and an instant-read thermometer inserted in center reads 170°F (75°C). Let cool 10 minutes before transferring to a platter or slicing. Makes 6 to 8 servings.

Chicken—Peanut Butter Loaf

This creation borrows from the flavors of Indonesia.

1 pound ground chicken
1/2 cup coconut milk
1/4 cup creamy peanut butter
1 egg, lightly beaten
1/2 cup dry bread crumbs
2 tablespoons soy sauce
1 tablespoon grated lemon zest
1 serrano or jalapeño chile, minced
2 garlic cloves, minced
2 teaspoons ground coriander
Salt and freshly ground pepper

Preheat oven to 350°F (175°C). Grease an 8″ × 4″ loaf pan. Combine chicken, coconut milk, peanut butter, egg, bread crumbs, soy sauce, lemon zest, chile, garlic, coriander, salt, and pepper in a medium-size bowl. Transfer chicken mixture to loaf pan.

Bake about 40 minutes or until an instant-read thermometer inserted in center of loaf reads 170°F (75°C). Let stand in pan 10 minutes. Makes 4 servings.

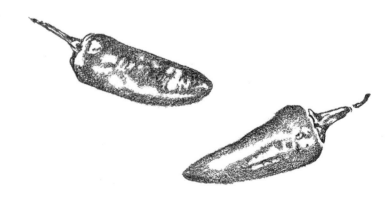

Turkey & Stuffing Loaf

This is Thanksgiving dinner in a loaf.

2 tablespoons butter or margarine
1 cup finely chopped onion
1 cup finely chopped celery
1 garlic clove, minced
1 pound ground turkey
2 cups 1-inch bread cubes
2 cups coarsely crumbled cornbread
1/2 cup white wine or apple juice
1 egg, lightly beaten
1 teaspoon dried leaf basil
1 teaspoon dried leaf thyme
Hot pepper sauce
Salt and freshly ground pepper

Preheat oven to 350°F (175°C). Grease a 9″ × 5″ loaf pan. Melt butter in a medium-size skillet over medium heat. Add onion, celery, and garlic and cook until softened.

Combine onion mixture, turkey, bread cubes, cornbread, wine, egg, basil, thyme, hot pepper sauce, salt, and pepper in a large bowl. Transfer turkey mixture to loaf pan.

Bake about 40 minutes or until an instant-read thermometer inserted in center of loaf reads 170°F (75°C). Let stand in pan 10 minutes. Makes 4 servings.

Seafood Loaves

Everyone is familiar with canned salmon loaf, but fresh fish and sea-food can be turned into elegant and delicious loaves that will catch many compliments. Even nonfish eaters may find themselves intrigued by fish when it is combined with shellfish and fresh herbs.

Fish is naturally low in fat, and most of the recipes add ingredients that enhance the flavor without adding lots of extra calories.

Take advantage of the natural colors of the fish and shellfish to make combinations that are attractive as well as complementary in taste. Feel free to experiment with whatever is the freshest in the market and use as a substitute for one of the fish called for in the recipe. I am always reminded of a friend who asked for my recipe for a fish stew that I had served at a dinner party she attended. She made my stew with a different fish—because that was what the market had—and the result was an equally good but different dish.

Salmon & Scallop Loaf

When you slice the loaf, the creamy white of the scallops stands out against the pink salmon.

About 2 pounds salmon steaks
2 tablespoons dry seasoned bread crumbs
1/4 cup white wine
1/4 cup half-and-half
2 eggs, lightly beaten
1 tablespoon minced chives
1 tablespoon chopped flat-leaf parsley
Salt and freshly ground pepper
About 6 ounces sea scallops

Preheat oven to 350°F (175°C). Grease an 8″ × 4″ nonstick loaf pan.

Finely chop salmon with a knife or food processor. Add bread crumbs, wine, half-and-half, eggs, chives, parsley, salt, and pepper.

Spoon half of salmon mixture into prepared pan. Arrange two rows of scallops down the center of loaf, pressing lightly into salmon mixture. Top scallops with remaining salmon mixture and smooth top.

Place loaf pan in a baking pan. Add enough hot water to come halfway up sides of loaf pan. Bake about 30 minutes or until loaf is firm and salmon is opaque. Let cool in pan 10 minutes. Drain off any liquid and turn out loaf onto a plate. Makes 4 servings.

Crab-stuffed Sole Ring

*Elegant enough for the most important dinner party, the crab and artichoke hearts fill
the delicate sole with interesting flavors and textures.*

1 (14-oz.) can artichoke hearts, drained and rinsed
1 tablespoon finely chopped green onion
1 tablespoon chopped flat-leaf parsley
1/4 cup seasoned dry bread crumbs
8 ounces crabmeat, picked over and flaked
About 12 ounces sole fillets
Salt and freshly ground pepper
Juice of 1/2 lime

Preheat oven to 350°F (175°C). Butter an 8-inch ring mold.

Process artichoke hearts in a food processor until coarsely chopped. Add onion, parsley, bread crumbs, and crabmeat. Process to combine. Set aside.

Arrange sole fillets in mold, overlapping slightly and allowing ends to extend over edges of pan. Season with salt and pepper. Spoon artichoke mixture evenly over fillets, pressing down slightly. Arrange ends of fillets over stuffing. Squeeze lime juice over fillets.

Place mold in a baking pan. Add enough hot water to come halfway up sides of mold. Bake 20 minutes or until fish turns from translucent to opaque. Let stand in mold 10 minutes. Drain off any liquid. Makes 4 servings.

Note

Letting a loaf stand in the pan before turning it out allows the loaf to absorb some of the juices that may be in the pan and also to firm before slicing.

Crab au Gratin Loaf

This loaf is flecked with colorful bits of tomato, parsley, and chives.
Serve with Cheese Sauce (page 120).

3 tablespoons butter or margarine
3 tablespoons all-purpose flour
1 cup milk
1 pound crabmeat, picked over and flaked
1 medium-size tomato, peeled and finely chopped
1 egg, lightly beaten
2 tablespoons dry seasoned bread crumbs
2 tablespoons chopped flat-leaf parsley
2 tablespoons snipped chives
2 tablespoons dry sherry
Hot pepper sauce to taste
Salt and freshly ground pepper

Preheat oven to 400°F (205°C). Butter an 8″ × 4″ loaf pan. Melt butter in a medium-size saucepan over medium heat. Stir in flour; cook, stirring, until bubbly. Stir in milk; cook, stirring, until thickened and floury taste is gone.

Stir in crabmeat, tomato, egg, bread crumbs, parsley, chives, sherry, hot pepper sauce, salt, and pepper. Transfer mixture to loaf pan.

Bake about 30 minutes or until top is browned and loaf is firm. Serve with Cheese Sauce (page 120). Makes 4 servings.

Variation

Substitute any flaked, cooked white fish for the crabmeat.

Deviled Crab Loaf

Easier to make than crab cakes, but just as good. Serve with fresh asparagus.

1 pound crabmeat, picked over
1/4 cup diced onion
1/4 cup diced red bell pepper
3 cups fresh bread crumbs
1/2 cup mayonnaise
1 tablespoon Dijon mustard
1 egg, lightly beaten
1/2 teaspoon dried leaf tarragon
1/8 teaspoon red (cayenne) pepper
1/4 teaspoon salt
Lemon wedges to serve

Preheat oven to 350°F (175°C). Butter an 8″ × 4″ nonstick loaf pan. Combine crabmeat, onion, bell pepper, and bread crumbs in a medium-size bowl.

Beat mayonnaise, mustard, egg, tarragon, cayenne, and salt together in a small bowl. Stir mayonnaise mixture into crabmeat mixture.

Spoon crab mixture into prepared pan. Place loaf pan in a baking pan. Add enough hot water to come halfway up sides of loaf pan. Bake 40 minutes or until loaf is set. Let stand in pan 10 minutes. Serve with lemon wedges. Makes about 4 servings.

Smoked Fish & Potato Loaf

The smokiness of the fish blends well with the potatoes and mushrooms in this loaf.

1 large russet potato, cut into 1-1/2-inch pieces
3 tablespoons butter or margarine
1-1/2 cups chopped onions
2 garlic cloves, minced
4 ounces fresh mushrooms, finely chopped
8 ounces smoked fish, such as alder-smoked salmon, halibut, trout, or whitefish, etc., flaked
2 eggs, slightly beaten
2 tablespoons dry bread crumbs
1 tablespoon chopped parsley
1 teaspoon dried dill weed
1 teaspoon salt
Freshly ground pepper

Preheat oven to 350°F (175°C). Grease a 9″ × 5″ nonstick loaf pan. Cook potato in salted water until tender. Drain and mash in a large bowl.

Melt butter in a medium-size skillet. Add onions and garlic and cook until softened. Add mushrooms and cook until moisture evaporates.

Add mushroom mixture, fish, eggs, bread crumbs, parsley, dill, salt, and pepper to potato in bowl. Mix until combined. Transfer mixture to loaf pan. Place loaf pan in a larger baking pan. Add enough hot water to come halfway up sides of loaf pan.

Bake about 40 minutes or until firm. Let stand in pan 10 minutes. Makes about 4 servings.

Trout Layered with Smoked Fish & Watercress

The smoky flavor of the fish blends well with the peppery watercress.

1 cup packed watercress, large stems removed
4 to 6 ounces smoked fish, such as halibut, whitefish, or alder-smoked salmon
2 eggs, lightly beaten
1/4 cup cracker crumbs
2 tablespoons fresh lemon juice
Salt and freshly ground pepper
6 trout fillets
Lemon wedges to serve

Preheat oven to 350°F (175°C). Grease an 8″ × 4″ loaf pan. Line bottom of pan with foil, extending foil over ends of pan, and grease foil. Add watercress to food processor; process until minced. Cut smoked fish into 2-inch pieces. Add fish pieces to watercress in food processor and process until minced. Transfer to a bowl. Combine eggs, cracker crumbs, lemon juice, salt, and pepper in a medium-size bowl. Stir in smoked fish mixture.

Line bottom of loaf pan with 2 trout fillets (don't worry if they don't completely cover bottom). Spoon one-third watercress mixture over trout and smooth top. Repeat with remaining trout fillets and watercress mixture, ending with 2 trout fillets.

Cover loaf with foil. Place loaf pan in a larger baking pan. Add enough hot water to come halfway up sides of loaf pan. Bake about 40 minutes or until loaf is firm. Let stand 10 minutes. Drain off any liquid. Turn out onto a serving plate and remove foil. Serve with lemon wedges. Makes 4 servings.

Variation

If there is a fisherperson among your family and friends, this is even more attractive made with salmon-colored lake trout.

Scallop- & Dill-Topped Tuna

The dill and scallops add a delicious, and pretty, accent to the fresh tuna steaks.

1 tablespoon olive oil
1/2 cup chopped green onions
4 ounces fresh mushrooms, finely chopped
1/2 red bell pepper, finely chopped
8 ounces bay or sea scallops, well drained
1 egg, lightly beaten
1/4 cup fresh bread crumbs
1/4 cup chopped fresh dill or 1 tablespoon dried dill weed
Salt and freshly ground black pepper
About 12 ounces tuna steaks, cut 1/2 inch thick

Preheat oven to 350°F (175°C). Grease a 9″ × 5″ loaf pan. Heat olive oil in a medium-size skillet over medium heat. Add green onions, mushrooms, and bell pepper and cook until softened.

Process scallops in a food processor until minced. Add egg and bread crumbs; process to combine. Add mushroom mixture, dill, salt, and pepper and process just to combine.

Line bottom of loaf pan with tuna, overlapping if necessary. Spoon scallop mixture over tuna and smooth top.

Cover loaf with foil. Place loaf pan in a larger baking pan. Add enough hot water to come halfway up sides of loaf pan. Bake about 40 minutes or until firm. Let stand 10 minutes. Drain off any liquid. Turn out onto a serving plate. Makes 4 to 6 servings.

Tuna & Tofu Loaf

Tofu is high in protein but contains no cholesterol, making it the perfect addition to a low-cholesterol, low-saturated-fat diet.

2 tablespoons butter or margarine
1 small green bell pepper, finely chopped
1 small onion, finely chopped
1 garlic clove, minced
2 tablespoons all-purpose flour
1 cup low-fat or regular milk
1 tablespoon Dijon mustard
1 (10.5-oz.) package firm tofu, drained and crumbled
1 (6-1/8-oz.) can light tuna, drained and flaked
1 cup fresh bread crumbs
2 eggs, lightly beaten

Preheat oven to 350°F (175°C). Grease a 9″ × 5″ nonstick loaf pan. Melt butter in a large skillet over medium heat. Add bell pepper, onion, and garlic and cook until vegetables are softened.

Sprinkle flour over vegetables and stir to combine. Add milk and cook, whisking constantly, until mixture comes to a boil and thickens. Stir in mustard. Cool slightly. Stir in tofu, tuna, bread crumbs, and eggs.

Transfer mixture to loaf pan and smooth top. Bake 1 hour or until loaf is browned. Let stand in pan 10 minutes. Makes 4 to 6 servings.

Salmon & Cabbage Strudel

Always keep the sheets of phyllo pastry covered; otherwise they will dry out quickly and break when you work with them.

2 tablespoons butter or margarine
1 large onion, chopped
4 cups chopped cabbage
1 (3-oz.) package regular or light cream cheese, softened
1 cup shredded Swiss cheese (4 ounces)
4 ounces smoked salmon, finely chopped
2 eggs, lightly beaten
1-1/2 teaspoons dried dill weed
1 teaspoon salt
Freshly ground pepper
10 phyllo pastry sheets
Nonstick cooking spray

Preheat oven to 375°F (190°C). Grease a baking sheet. Melt butter in a large skillet over low heat. Add onion and cabbage. Cover and cook, stirring occasionally, until crisp-tender. Cool slightly.

Combine cream cheese, Swiss cheese, salmon, eggs, dill, salt, and pepper in a large bowl. Add vegetable mixture and stir to combine.

Place 1 phyllo sheet on a work surface; cover remaining sheets with plastic wrap to prevent drying. Spray phyllo sheet with nonstick cooking spray and top with another sheet of pastry. Continue with remaining pastry sheets, spraying each with nonstick cooking spray.

Spoon filling in center of pastry, leaving a 3-inch border on all sides. Fold ends over filling, then fold in sides. Carefully transfer to baking sheet. Bake about 30 minutes or until golden brown. Makes about 6 servings.

Easy Salmon Loaf

Canned salmon is a staple in many kitchens. A can of salmon can easily be made into a healthy, appetizing loaf. This one contains no eggs to keep the cholesterol level low.

1 (15-1/2-oz.) can red salmon
1 cup fresh bread crumbs
2 tablespoons wheat germ
1 celery stalk, finely chopped
2 tablespoons chopped flat-leaf parsley
1 teaspoon dried leaf tarragon
Salt and freshly ground pepper
Dill Sauce (page 120)

Preheat oven to 350°F (175°C). Grease an 8″ × 4″ loaf pan. Pour salmon and liquid into a medium-size bowl; flake salmon and discard skin and large bones.

Stir in bread crumbs, wheat germ, celery, parsley, tarragon, salt, and pepper.

Transfer to loaf pan. Bake about 40 minutes or until lightly browned. Let stand in pan 10 minutes. Serve with Dill Sauce (page 120). Makes 4 servings.

Steamed Shrimp Loaf

A Chinese steamer works well for this loaf, but any large steamer basket will work.

Yeast Dough (see below)
2 cups bean sprouts
2 cups finely chopped Napa cabbage
2 dried Chinese mushrooms, soaked in water 30 minutes
1 pound shelled shrimp, cooked and coarsely chopped
4 green onions, finely chopped
1 egg, lightly beaten
2 tablespoons sherry
1 teaspoon grated gingerroot
Salt and freshly ground pepper
Dipping Sauce (see below)

Yeast Dough:

1 (1/4-oz.) package active dry yeast
1 tablespoon sugar
1/4 cup lukewarm water
1 cup milk
3 cups all-purpose flour
1/2 teaspoon salt

Dipping Sauce:

1/2 cup low-sodium soy sauce
1/3 cup seasoned wine vinegar
2 garlic cloves, minced
2 tablespoons minced green onion tops
2 tablespoons minced cilantro
1 teaspoon chile paste

Prepare dough. Cook bean sprouts and cabbage in boiling water 2 minutes, immediately drain, and place in ice water. Drain well. Drain mushrooms, discard stems, and chop caps. Combine bean sprouts, cabbage, mushrooms, shrimp, green onions, egg, sherry, gingerroot, salt, and pepper in a medium-size bowl.

Roll out dough into a 16-inch round. Line a 10-inch bamboo steamer basket with cheesecloth. Fold dough in quarters and place in cheesecloth-lined basket. Unfold dough and let edges extend over edge of basket. Spoon shrimp mixture in center of dough. Moisten edge of dough and bring to center, pleating dough and twisting to seal. Cover with plastic wrap and let rise in a warm place about 30 minutes or until doubled in bulk.

Remove plastic wrap and place basket over boiling water. Cover basket with lid. Steam 1 hour, adding water as needed, or until dough springs back when lightly pressed. Prepare sauce. Cut loaf into wedges to serve and serve with sauce. Makes 6 servings.

Dough

Dissolve yeast and sugar in water in the bowl of an electric mixer. Let stand until foamy, about 5 minutes. Add milk, 2 cups of the flour, and salt. Beat until smooth. Add enough remaining flour to make a soft dough. Knead with the dough hook about 10 minutes or until smooth. Cover bowl and let rise in a warm place until doubled in bulk, about 45 minutes. Punch down dough and shape into a ball.

Dipping Sauce

Combine all ingredients in a small bowl.

Variation

Steamed Shrimp & Pork Loaf

Reduce shrimp to 8 ounces. Add 8 ounces cooked drained ground pork to shrimp mixture.

Tuna & Egg Loaf

Similar to a warm tuna salad but even better, this is quick and easy to make.

1 (14-oz.) can light tuna, drained
2 hard-cooked eggs, finely chopped
1/4 cup mayonnaise
1 cup fresh bread crumbs
3 green onions with tops, finely chopped
1 tablespoon capers, rinsed and drained
1 tablespoon finely chopped flat-leaf parsley
Salt and freshly ground pepper

Preheat oven to 350°F (175°C). Grease an 8″ × 4″ loaf pan. Break up tuna into small pieces. Combine tuna, eggs, mayonnaise, bread crumbs, green onions, capers, parsley, salt, and pepper in a medium-size bowl. Transfer mixture to loaf pan and smooth top.

Bake about 40 minutes or until loaf is browned. Let cool in pan 10 minutes. Makes 4 servings.

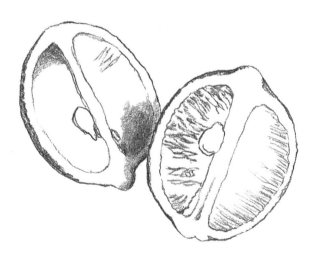

Fresh Salmon & Fennel Loaf

The delicate anise flavor of the fennel complements the salmon.

About 2 pounds salmon fillets
1/4 cup finely chopped fennel bulb and top
1/2 cup half-and-half
1/2 cup fresh bread crumbs
1 egg, lightly beaten
Salt and freshly ground pepper

Preheat oven to 350°F (175°C). Grease an 8″ × 4″ loaf pan. Finely chop salmon with a knife. Combine salmon, fennel, half-and-half, bread crumbs, egg, salt, and pepper in a medium-size bowl.

Transfer mixture to loaf pan. Set loaf pan in a baking pan. Add enough hot water to come halfway up sides of loaf pan. Bake about 20 minutes or until loaf is firm. Remove from water. Let cool in pan 5 minutes. Drain off any liquid and turn out onto a plate. Makes 4 servings.

Steamed Salmon & Halibut Mousse with Leek Sauce

Pretty and delicious, these fish loaves are heart healthy as well.

Leek Sauce (page 121)
3/4 pound halibut
1 tablespoon chopped flat-leaf parsley
1/4 teaspoon dried leaf tarragon
Salt and freshly ground pepper
1 egg white
1/2 pound salmon fillet, thinly sliced diagonally

Prepare Leek Sauce and keep warm. Grease 4 (4-1/2″ × 2-1/2″) loaf pans. Cut halibut into 2-inch pieces. Process halibut in a food processor until finely chopped. Transfer to a bowl. Add parsley, tarragon, salt, and pepper. Beat egg white in a small bowl until stiff but not dry. Fold egg white into halibut mixture.

Line bottom and sides of loaf pans with salmon. Spoon halibut mixture into salmon-lined pans and smooth tops.

Place loaves on a rack over simmering water. Cover and steam about 10 minutes or until fish are opaque. Remove from water and let stand 5 minutes. Spoon some sauce on 4 dinner plates. Drain off any liquid from loaves and invert onto pools of sauce. Makes 4 servings.

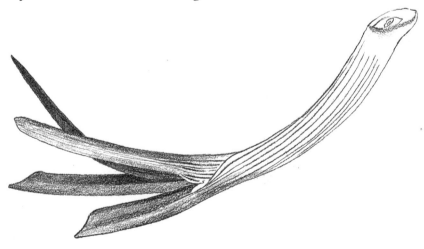

Potato-filled Fresh Tuna & Shrimp Loaf

Add a steamed green vegetable such as broccoli or asparagus and perhaps
a tomato salad to complete this elegant meal.

1 pound fresh tuna steaks
4 very large shrimp, shelled and butterflied
2 pounds potatoes, cooked
Milk
1/4 cup chopped flat-leaf parsley
Pinch of saffron threads soaked in 1 tablespoon white wine or water
1 roasted garlic head (page 114), cloves removed and mashed
Salt and freshly ground pepper

Preheat oven to 350°F (175°C). Grease an 8-inch ring mold. Cut tuna crosswise into about 1/2-inch-thick slices. Arrange shrimp equal distances apart in ring mold. Line remainder of ring with tuna slices, fitting in pieces to patch any holes. Refrigerate while preparing filling.

Drain potatoes and mash. Stir in just enough milk to reach a consistency a little stiffer than that of regular mashed potatoes. Stir in parsley, saffron with wine, roasted garlic, salt, and pepper.

Carefully fill center of ring with potato mixture. Place ring in a baking pan. Add enough hot water to come halfway up sides of ring. Bake about 10 minutes or until tuna is opaque and center is hot. Remove from water. Let cool in pan 5 minutes. Drain off any liquid and turn out ring onto a plate.

To serve, cut between shrimp so that each serving has one shrimp in its center. Makes 4 servings.

Asparagus & Smoked Salmon Sandwich Loaf

*This makes impressive sandwiches to serve with afternoon tea. When the loaf is sliced,
the green rounds of the asparagus stalks and the pink salmon form an attractive
design with the creamy cheese and brown of the bread.*

8 ounces light or regular cream cheese, softened
1/4 cup light sour cream
1 tablespoon capers, drained
1/2 teaspoon prepared horseradish
1 teaspoon Dijon mustard
1/4 cup pimiento-stuffed olives, coarsely chopped
1 teaspoon fresh lemon juice
Freshly ground pepper
1 (1-lb.) unsliced whole-grain-bread loaf
1 pound fresh asparagus, cooked until crisp-tender
4 ounces smoked salmon, thinly sliced
Fresh dill or fennel sprigs to garnish

Beat cream cheese and sour cream until light and fluffy in a medium-size bowl. Divide mixture, placing half in another bowl. Stir capers, horseradish, and mustard into half of cheese mixture. Stir olives, lemon juice, and pepper into remaining half.

Cut crust from loaf, then cut loaf lengthwise into 4 long slices. Spread a thin layer of cream cheese with olives over top of bottom bread slice. Arrange asparagus over cream cheese mixture, alternating tops and ends of stalks. Spread a thin layer of cream cheese with olives over bottom of next slice and place over asparagus.

Spread top of slice with a thin layer of cream cheese with capers. Arrange smoked salmon over cream cheese mixture. Spread bottom of next slice with a thin layer of cream cheese with capers and place over salmon.

Spread a thin layer of cream cheese with olives over top of bread slice. Arrange stalks of asparagus over cream cheese mixture, alternating tops and ends of spears. Spread a thin layer of cream cheese with olives over bottom of next slice and place over asparagus. Spread top of loaf with remaining cheese with capers. Arrange dill sprigs over top. Refrigerate uncovered about 1 hour to firm. Cover loosely with plastic wrap if not serving after 1 hour and refrigerate up to 8 hours. To serve, cut with a serrated knife into thin slices. Makes 10 or 12 slices.

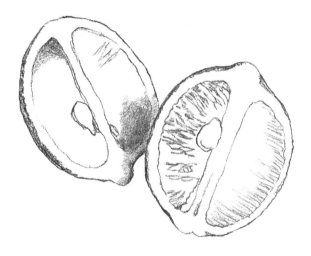

Salmon & White Bean Loaf

Easy to prepare from your emergency shelf supplies. You'll be surprised at the way the beans change a standard salmon loaf into something special.

---

1 (15-1/2-oz.) can pink salmon
1 (15-oz.) can cannellini (white kidney) beans, drained and rinsed
1 (7-oz.) jar roasted red bell peppers, drained and chopped
3 tablespoons dry bread crumbs
1/4 cup chopped fresh fennel tops or 2 tablespoons dried fennel
1 tablespoon chopped flat-leaf parsley
Salt and freshly ground black pepper

Preheat oven to 350°F (175°C). Grease a 9″ × 5″ loaf pan. Drain salmon and discard bones and skin. Flake large pieces of salmon. Process beans in a food processor until pureed. Add salmon and process until coarsely chopped.

Transfer salmon mixture to a bowl. Stir in bell peppers, bread crumbs, fennel, parsley, salt, and pepper. Spoon into prepared pan. Bake about 1 hour or until browned. Makes 4 to 6 servings.

Variation

For a firmer loaf, add 1 tablespoon more bread crumbs and 1 beaten egg to salmon mixture.

Layered Potato, Onion & Chile Loaf with Salmon

Perfect for brunch or lunch—serve with a mixed green salad.

1-1/4 pounds potatoes, baked until partially cooked, thinly sliced crosswise
1 large sweet onion, very thinly sliced crosswise, separated into rings
6 mild green chiles, roasted, peeled, and cut into strips, or 6 canned green chiles, cut into strips
4 to 6 ounces smoked salmon, thinly sliced
8 ounces (2 cups) shredded mozzarella cheese
6 eggs, lightly beaten
6 tablespoons milk
2 tablespoons all-purpose flour
Salt and freshly ground pepper to taste

Preheat oven to 350°F (175°). Grease a 9″ × 5″ nonstick loaf pan. Alternate layers of potatoes, onion, chiles, salmon, and cheese in loaf pan, starting and ending with potatoes.

Beat eggs, milk, flour, salt, and pepper in a large bowl until light and lemon-colored. Pour egg mixture over loaf.

Bake 1 hour or until egg mixture is set in center. Let stand in pan 10 minutes. Makes about 6 servings.

Vegetable Loaves

This chapter certainly proves that loaves do not have to contain meat to taste delicious. Actually some of my favorite loaves start with several kinds of vegetables. Some good choices for vegetable loaves are artichoke hearts, broccoli, carrots, cauliflower, leeks, mushrooms, onions, spinach, and zucchini. Vegetables can be easily and quickly chopped in batches in a food processor. Cooking the vegetables in a little olive oil before adding to the other ingredients brings out the flavors and reduces the amount of moisture so you don't have a "wet" loaf.

Add cheeses, bread crumbs, and eggs to the vegetables and great things happen. The eggs can even be egg whites or egg substitutes if you're watching cholesterol.

Many of the vegetable loaves are as delicious for appetizers as for main dishes. Several travel well and can be served cold, so they are perfect picnic fare.

Tofu-Broccoli Loaf

Tofu (soybean curd), is low in fat and contains no cholesterol. Relatively bland in flavor,
it takes on the tastes of the ingredients that are added to it.

2 tablespoons olive oil
1 cup finely chopped onion
2 garlic cloves, minced
2 (10.5-oz.) packages firm tofu, drained and crumbled
1-3/4 cups fresh whole-wheat bread crumbs
1/4 cup wheat germ
1 cup finely chopped broccoli
2 eggs, lightly beaten
2 tablespoons chopped fresh flat-leaf parsley
1 teaspoon dried leaf marjoram
1 teaspoon salt
Freshly ground pepper
1/2 cup roasted pumpkin seeds (optional)

Preheat oven to 350°F (175°C). Grease a 9″ × 5″ loaf pan. Heat oil in a medium-size skillet over medium heat. Add onion and garlic and cook until softened.

Combine onion mixture, tofu, bread crumbs, wheat germ, broccoli, eggs, parsley, marjoram, salt, pepper, and pumpkin seeds, if using, in a large bowl. Transfer mixture to loaf pan and pack lightly.

Bake about 1 hour or until browned. Let stand in pan 10 minutes before cutting. Makes 4 to 6 servings.

Bean & Nut Loaf

Use your favorite beans and nuts in this easy loaf. A salsa would go well with this.

2 cups cooked pinto beans or 1 (15-oz.) can pinto beans, drained and rinsed
1 medium-size green bell pepper, finely chopped
1 medium-size onion, finely chopped
1 small carrot, finely shredded
1 celery stalk, finely chopped
4 ounces walnuts or pecans, finely chopped (1 cup)
1 cup fresh bread crumbs
1 egg, lightly beaten
1 teaspoon dried leaf basil
1/4 teaspoon dried leaf thyme
Salt and freshly ground black pepper

Preheat oven to 350°F (175°C). Grease a 9″ × 5″ nonstick loaf pan. Process beans in a food processor until pureed; set aside.

Heat olive oil in a large skillet over medium heat. Add bell pepper, onion, carrot, and celery. Cook until vegetables are softened, stirring occasionally.

Add beans, nuts, bread crumbs, egg, basil, thyme, salt, and black pepper to vegetables. Transfer to loaf pan and smooth top.

Bake about 40 minutes or until golden brown. Let stand in pan 10 minutes. Makes 4 to 6 servings.

 Note

Nuts can be chopped or coarsely ground, in small batches, in a food processor or nut grinder using the coarse blade. Do not overprocess nuts, or they will be too fine.

Two-Bean Loaf

Choose any two different beans for this loaf.

2 cup cooked navy beans or 1 (15-oz.) can navy beans, drained and rinsed
2 cups cooked red kidney beans or 1 (15-oz.) can red kidney beans, drained and rinsed
1 tablespoon olive oil
1 large onion, finely chopped
1 large green bell pepper, finely chopped
1 large carrot, finely shredded
1 celery stalk, minced
1 cup fresh bread crumbs
1 egg, lightly beaten
1 tablespoon chopped fresh flat-leaf parsley
1/2 teaspoon dried savory
Salt and freshly ground black pepper

Preheat oven to 350°F (175°C). Grease a 9″ × 5″ nonstick loaf pan. Process beans together in a food processor until pureed; set aside.

Heat olive oil in a large skillet over medium heat. Add onion, bell pepper, carrot, and celery. Cook until vegetables are softened.

Add beans, bread crumbs, egg, parsley, savory, salt, and black pepper to vegetables. Transfer to loaf pan and smooth top.

Bake about 30 minutes or until golden brown. Let stand in pan 10 minutes. Makes 4 servings.

Variation

Process beans separately in a food processor until pureed. Mix all remaining ingredients together. Divide in half and add half to pureed navy beans and half to pureed kidney beans. Add kidney bean mixture to loaf pan, pack lightly, and smooth top. Repeat with navy bean mixture.

Curried Lentil & Bulgur Loaf

The lentils and bulgur give this loaf a Middle Eastern flavor.

1-1/4 cups lentils
4 cups water
3/4 cup boiling water
1/2 cup bulgur
1 tablespoon olive oil
1 small onion, finely chopped
1 garlic clove, minced
1 egg, lightly beaten
1 cup finely chopped tomato
1 jalapeño chile (optional), minced
1 tablespoon curry powder
1 teaspoon ground coriander
1 teaspoon salt
Freshly ground pepper

Combine lentils and the 4 cups water in a medium-size saucepan. Bring to a boil; boil 10 minutes. Reduce heat, cover, and simmer about 30 minutes or until lentils are tender. Add more water if needed. Most of the liquid should evaporate.

While lentils are cooking, pour boiling water over bulgur in a small bowl. Let stand about 30 minutes or until most of water is absorbed. Drain any water from lentils and bulgur.

Preheat oven to 350°F (175°C). Grease an 8″ × 4″ loaf pan. Heat olive oil in a medium-size skillet over medium heat. Add onion and garlic and cook until softened. Combine lentils, bulgur, onion mixture, egg, tomato, chile, if using, curry powder, coriander, salt, and pepper in a medium-size bowl. Spoon into loaf pan and pack lightly.

Bake about 50 minutes or until loaf is browned and has firmed. Makes 4 servings.

Roasted Vegetable Loaf

A great dish to make the night before to take with you on a picnic. The bread absorbs the delicious juices from the vegetables.

1 large sweet onion, cut into 1-inch pieces
2 medium-size white rose potatoes, cut into 1-inch cubes
6 tablespoons olive oil
1 (1-lb.) eggplant, cut into 1-inch cubes
1 red bell pepper, cut into 1-inch pieces
2 plum tomatoes, cut into 1-inch pieces
2 small zucchini, cut into 1/2-inch rounds
1 tablespoon chopped fresh basil or 1 teaspoon dried leaf basil
Salt and freshly ground pepper
1 large loaf French bread

Preheat oven to 425°F (220°C). Toss onion and potatoes with 2 tablespoons of the olive oil. Spread in a 13″ × 9″ baking pan. Bake 30 minutes. Toss eggplant, bell pepper, tomatoes, and zucchini with remaining olive oil. Add to onion and potatoes and toss to combine. Add basil and season with salt and pepper.

Bake 30 minutes, stirring occasionally, or until all vegetables are just tender and browned.

Cut a thin slice off top of loaf; set aside. Remove soft interior of loaf with a fork, leaving a 1-inch-thick wall. Spoon vegetables into loaf and replace top. Wrap in plastic wrap and refrigerate overnight. To serve, cut loaf into thick slices. Makes about 6 servings.

Variation

Sprinkle freshly grated Parmesan cheese or shredded Monterey Jack cheese between layers of vegetables as you fill the loaf.

Artichoke, Spinach & Feta Round

This blend of flavors reminds me of having lunch in Greece under vines laden with grapes on a late summer day. This is a great appetizer or main dish with a glass of dry white wine.

Flaky Crust (pages 96–97)
1 (6-oz.) jar marinated artichoke hearts, well drained
4 ounces feta cheese, coarsely crumbled
1/4 cup freshly grated Parmesan cheese
1 (10-oz.) package frozen chopped spinach, thawed and squeezed dry or 1 (10-oz.) package fresh
    spinach, cooked, squeezed dry, and chopped
1/4 cup chopped sun-dried tomatoes
1 medium-size tomato, finely chopped
1/2 red bell pepper, roasted, peeled, and finely chopped
1 large garlic clove, minced
1 tablespoon dry bread crumbs
2 teaspoons dried leaf basil
1/2 teaspoon dried leaf oregano
1/8 teaspoon freshly grated nutmeg
Freshly ground black pepper
Milk

Prepare dough for crust, omitting oregano. Preheat oven to 400°F (205°C). Grease an 8-inch springform pan.

Process artichoke hearts in a food processor until coarsely chopped. Transfer artichokes to a large bowl. Add cheeses, spinach, sun-dried tomatoes, fresh tomato, bell pepper, garlic, bread crumbs, basil, oregano, nutmeg, and black pepper. Mix until combined.

Roll out two-thirds of dough into a 12-inch circle. Use dough to line springform pan. Spoon spinach mixture into dough. Roll out remaining dough into a 9-inch circle. Place dough over filling. Fold edges over and crimp edges to seal. Cut vents to allow steam to escape. Brush with milk.

Bake about 45 minutes or until golden brown. Cool in pan 10 minutes. Remove rim of pan. Cut into wedges. Makes 8 servings.

Pasta in the Round

This is an intriguing way to serve pasta in wedges! Accompany the wedges with a tomato sauce, if desired. Because of its density, the loaf stays warm a long time.

Flaky Crust (see below)
1/4 cup butter or margarine
1/4 cup finely chopped onion
3 tablespoons all-purpose flour
2 cups milk
1/4 teaspoon freshly grated nutmeg
Salt and freshly ground pepper
1 cup shredded smoked or regular mozzarella cheese (4 ounces)
1/4 cup grated Parmesan cheese
1 (9-oz.) package fresh cheese-filled spinach tortellini, cooked according to pasta directions and drained
4 ounces fresh mushrooms, sliced
1 medium-size tomato, chopped
1/2 cup sliced ripe olives
Milk

Flaky Crust:

2-1/4 cups all-purpose flour
1/2 teaspoon salt
1 teaspoon dried leaf oregano
3/4 cup butter or margarine, chilled
1 egg, lightly beaten
About 1/4 cup ice water

Prepare dough for crust. Preheat oven to 400°F (205°C). Grease an 8-inch springform pan.

Melt butter in a saucepan over medium heat. Add onion and cook until softened. Stir in flour and cook until bubbly. Stir in milk and cook, stirring, until thickened. Season with nutmeg, salt, and pepper. Stir in cheeses.

Combine tortellini, mushrooms, tomato, and olives in a large bowl. Pour cheese sauce over tortellini mixture.

Roll out two-thirds of dough into a 12-inch circle. Use dough to line springform pan. Spoon tortellini mixture into dough. Roll out remaining dough into a 9-inch circle. Place dough over filling. Fold over edges and crimp edges to seal. Cut vents to allow steam to escape. Brush with milk.

Bake about 45 minutes or until golden brown. Cool in pan 30 minutes. Remove rim of pan. Cut into wedges. Makes 8 servings.

Flaky Crust

Combine flour, salt, and oregano in a medium-size bowl. Cut in butter until mixture resembles coarse crumbs. Stir in egg and enough water to make a firm dough. Shape into a ball, cover with plastic wrap, and refrigerate 30 minutes.

Variation

Sausage & Pasta in the Round

Remove casings from two or three spicy Italian sausages. Cook in a skillet over medium heat, stirring to break up meat, until browned. Drain off fat and stir into pasta mixture.

Shrimp & Pasta in the Round

Add about 12 ounces cooked and shelled shrimp to pasta mixture.

Vegetable Loaf with Two Cheeses

This loaf is high in natural fiber and the cheeses bring out the flavor of the vegetables.

1 tablespoon olive oil
1 small sweet potato, peeled and shredded
2 cups finely chopped broccoli
1 cup shredded zucchini
1 cup finely chopped onion
1 large garlic clove, minced
1 cup cottage cheese, pressed through a sieve
1/4 cup freshly grated Parmesan cheese
1 cup fresh bread crumbs
2 eggs, lightly beaten
1 teaspoon dried leaf marjoram
1/8 teaspoon freshly grated nutmeg
Salt and freshly ground pepper

Preheat oven to 350°F (175°C). Grease a 9″ × 5″ nonstick loaf pan. Heat oil in a large skillet over low heat. Add sweet potato, broccoli, zucchini, onion, and garlic. Cook, stirring occasionally, until vegetables are softened and liquid evaporates.

Combine vegetable mixture, cottage cheese, Parmesan cheese, bread crumbs, eggs, marjoram, nutmeg, salt, and pepper in a large bowl. Spoon into loaf pan and pack lightly.

Bake about 50 minutes or until loaf is browned and firm. Makes 4 to 6 servings.

Variation

Substitute egg substitute or 4 egg whites for the eggs.

Note

If you don't have a nonstick pan, line the bottom of the pan with foil, extending foil over ends of pan, and grease foil. This helps remove the loaf from the pan without breaking it.

Mushroom Loaf

A friend of mine was convinced that this loaf contains meat—but it doesn't—and it has no cholesterol because it's made with egg whites. It's also excellent cold for a sandwich or appetizer.

2 tablespoons olive oil
1 pound fresh mushrooms, finely chopped
1 small onion, finely chopped
1 large carrot, shredded
1 large celery stalk, finely chopped
1/4 cup white wine or chicken broth
1 medium-size tomato, finely chopped
2 cups fresh whole-wheat bread crumbs
2 tablespoons wheat germ
2 egg whites, lightly beaten
1-1/2 teaspoons dried leaf basil
1/4 teaspoon dried leaf thyme
Dash hot pepper sauce
Salt and pepper

Preheat oven to 350°F (175°C). Grease a 9″ × 5″ loaf pan. Heat oil in a large skillet over medium heat. Add mushrooms, onion, carrot, and celery. Cook, stirring occasionally, until vegetables are softened and liquid evaporates. Add wine and cook until wine evaporates.

    Combine vegetable mixture, tomato, bread crumbs, wheat germ, egg whites, basil, thyme, hot pepper sauce, salt, and pepper in a large bowl. Spoon into loaf pan and pack lightly.

    Bake about 40 minutes or until browned and loaf has firmed. Makes 4 to 6 servings.

Note

The mushrooms, onion, carrot, and celery can all be chopped quickly in a food processor.

Vegetable-Cheese Strudel

Even kids will eat their vegetables when you serve them this way—
this recipe was kid-tested to prove it.

2 tablespoons butter or margarine
1 large onion, chopped
3 cups chopped cabbage
3 cups shredded carrots
1 large garlic clove, minced
1 cup cottage cheese
2 cups shredded Swiss cheese (8 ounces)
2 eggs, lightly beaten
1-1/2 teaspoons dried leaf basil
1/2 teaspoon dried leaf marjoram
1 teaspoon salt
Freshly ground pepper
10 phyllo pastry sheets
Nonstick cooking spray

Preheat oven to 375°F (190°C). Grease a baking sheet. Melt butter in a large skillet over low heat. Add onion, cover, and cook 5 minutes. Add cabbage, carrots, and garlic and stir to combine. Cover and cook, stirring occasionally, until crisp-tender. Cool slightly.

Combine cottage cheese, Swiss cheese, eggs, basil, marjoram, salt, and pepper in a large bowl. Add vegetable mixture and stir to combine.

Place 1 phyllo sheet on a work surface; cover remaining sheets with plastic wrap to prevent drying. Spray phyllo sheet with nonstick cooking spray and top with another sheet of pastry. Continue with remaining pastry sheets, spraying each with nonstick cooking spray.

Spoon filling in center of pastry, leaving a 3-inch border on all sides. Fold ends over filling, then fold in sides. Bake about 30 minutes or until golden brown. Makes about 6 servings.

Variations

Cutting down on cholesterol? Substitute 3 egg whites for the 2 whole eggs.

Brush phyllo sheets with melted butter or margarine instead of spraying with nonstick cooking spray. The pastry will be crisper—and, of course, contain more calories!

 Note

Dishes made with phyllo pastry are at their best when eaten just after baking. This can be assembled several hours in advance, covered with plastic wrap, and refrigerated until baking.

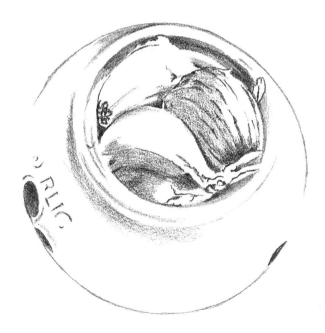

White Bean Loaf

Rich in healthy soluble fiber and full of flavor.

4 cups cooked butter beans (mature limas) or 2 (15-oz.) cans butter beans, drained and rinsed
1 tablespoon olive oil
1 large green bell pepper, finely chopped
1 medium-size onion, finely chopped
1 large carrot, finely shredded
1 garlic clove, minced
1 cup fresh bread crumbs
1 egg, lightly beaten
1 tablespoon chopped fresh flat-leaf parsley
1 teaspoon fresh rosemary, finely chopped
Salt and freshly ground black pepper

Preheat oven to 350°F (175°C). Grease a 9″ × 5″ nonstick loaf pan. Process beans in a food processor until pureed; set aside.

Heat olive oil in a large skillet over medium heat. Add bell pepper, onion, carrot, and garlic. Cook until vegetables are softened.

Add beans, bread crumbs, egg, parsley, rosemary, salt, and black pepper to vegetables. Transfer to loaf pan.

Bake about 30 minutes or until golden brown. Let stand in pan 10 minutes. Makes 4 servings.

Variation

Substitute any cooked or canned beans for the butter beans.

Pecan & Vegetable Loaf

Excellent hot or cold, this is ideal picnic fare for nonmeat eaters. This is one of my favorite loaves.

1 tablespoon olive oil
1 medium-size green bell pepper, finely chopped
1 medium-size onion, finely chopped
1 small carrot, finely shredded
1 medium-size tomato, diced
8 ounces pecans, finely chopped (2 cups)
2 cups fresh bread crumbs
1 egg, lightly beaten
1 teaspoon dried leaf basil
1 teaspoon finely chopped fresh rosemary or 3/4 teaspoon dried rosemary
Salt and freshly ground black pepper

Preheat oven to 350°F (175°C). Grease an 8″ × 4″ loaf pan. Heat olive oil in a large skillet over medium heat. Add bell pepper, onion, and carrot. Cook until vegetables are softened.

Add tomato, pecans, bread crumbs, egg, basil, rosemary, salt, and black pepper to vegetables. Transfer to loaf pan and pack lightly.

Bake about 40 minutes or until golden brown. Serve warm. Makes 4 servings.

Tofu-Spinach Loaf

Don't forget tofu when making loaves; it's high in protein and low in calories.
This is a light-textured loaf accented with the crunch of pine nuts.

2 tablespoons olive oil
1 cup chopped onion
2 garlic cloves, minced
2 (10.5-oz.) packages firm tofu, drained and crumbled
1 (10-oz.) package frozen chopped spinach, thawed and squeezed dry or 1 (10-oz.) package fresh
    spinach, cooked, squeezed dry, and chopped
1/4 cup dry bread crumbs
1/4 cup pine nuts
2 egg whites, lightly beaten
2 tablespoons chopped fresh flat-leaf parsley
1 teaspoon dried leaf basil
1 teaspoon salt
Freshly ground pepper

Preheat oven to 350° (175°C). Grease a 9″ × 5″ nonstick loaf pan. Heat oil in a medium-size skillet over medium heat. Add onion and garlic and cook until softened.

Combine onion mixture, tofu, spinach, bread crumbs, pine nuts, egg whites, parsley, basil, salt, and pepper in a large bowl. Transfer to loaf pan and pack lightly.

Bake about 1 hour or until browned. Let stand in pan 10 minutes before cutting. Makes 4 to 6 servings.

Variation

For a completely vegetarian loaf, omit egg whites. Loaf will be soft.

Potato-Spinach Loaf

The potatoes are accented by the mushrooms and spinach in this dill-flavored loaf.
I like to use unpeeled potatoes.

1 large russet potato, cut into 2-inch pieces
3 tablespoons butter, margarine, or olive oil
1-1/2 cups chopped onions
2 garlic cloves, minced
8 ounces fresh mushrooms, finely chopped
1 (10-oz.) package frozen chopped spinach, thawed and squeezed dry or 1 (10-oz.) package fresh
   spinach, cooked, squeezed dry, and chopped
2 eggs, lightly beaten
2 tablespoons dry bread crumbs
1 tablespoon chopped parsley
1 teaspoon dried dill weed
1 teaspoon salt
Freshly ground pepper

Preheat oven to 350°F (175°C). Grease a 9″ × 5″ nonstick loaf pan. Cook potato in salted water about 20 minutes or until tender. Drain and mash in a large bowl.

Melt butter in a medium-size skillet. Add onions and garlic and cook over medium heat until softened. Add mushrooms and cook until moisture evaporates.

Add spinach, eggs, bread crumbs, parsley, dill, salt, pepper, and mushroom mixture to potato in bowl. Mix until combined. Transfer mixture to loaf pan. Place loaf pan in a larger baking pan. Add enough hot water to come halfway up sides of loaf pan.

Bake about 50 minutes or until firm. Let stand in pan 10 minutes. Makes 4 servings.

Layered Vegetable Loaf with Roasted Garlic

The flavor is even better after the loaf cools to room temperature. You might want to roast the whole head of garlic and use the leftovers for garlic-scented olive oil or to add to salad dressings.

1 eggplant (about 1 pound)
4 large garlic cloves
4 eggs, lightly beaten
1/2 cup white wine or water
1/4 cup freshly grated Parmesan cheese
6 tablespoons Italian bread crumbs
1 teaspoon dried leaf basil
Hot pepper sauce
Salt and freshly ground black pepper
8 ounces zucchini, shredded
1/2 red bell pepper, sliced crosswise into thin rings
1/2 cup finely chopped onion
1 large Portbello mushroom cap, thinly sliced

Preheat oven to 350°F (175°C). Grease a 9″ × 5″ nonstick loaf pan. Place eggplant and unpeeled garlic in a baking pan. Bake about 1 hour or until eggplant is soft. Let eggplant and garlic cool. Cut eggplant crosswise into slices about 1/4 inch thick. Squeeze garlic out of skins and mash cloves.

Combine garlic, eggs, wine, cheese, bread crumbs, basil, hot pepper sauce, salt, and black pepper in a medium-size bowl.

Alternate layers of eggplant, zucchini, bell pepper, onion, and mushroom in loaf pan, making at least two layers of each. Pour egg mixture over layered vegetables.

Place loaf pan in a larger baking pan. Add enough water to come halfway up sides of loaf pan.

Bake about 1 hour or until liquid in center of loaf is set. Let cool in pan 10 minutes. Makes 4 to 6 servings.

Variation

Substitute 2 ounces sliced button mushrooms for the Portbello mushroom.

Broccoli, Cauliflower & Cheese Loaf

Cheese and broccoli always go wonderfully together.

1 head broccoli, separated into flowerets
1/2 head cauliflower, separated into flowerets
1 carrot, cut crosswise into 1/2-inch slices
2 green onions, minced
3 eggs, lightly beaten
2 tablespoons half-and-half
3 tablespoons dry bread crumbs
Salt and freshly ground pepper
2 cups shredded Cheddar cheese (8 ounces)

Preheat oven to 350°F (175°C). Grease a 9″ × 5″ nonstick loaf pan. Steam broccoli, cauliflower, and carrot until crisp-tender. Process broccoli and a few cauliflowerets in a food processor until finely chopped.

Combine chopped broccoli, green onions, eggs, half-and-half, 2 tablespoons bread crumbs, salt, and pepper in a medium-size bowl.

Sprinkle remaining bread crumbs in bottom of loaf pan. Layer remaining cauliflower, carrot, and cheese over crumbs. Pour egg mixture over vegetables and cheese. Place loaf pan in a large baking pan. Add enough water to come halfway up sides of loaf pan.

Bake about 1 hour or until liquid in center of loaf is set. Let cool in pan 10 minutes. Makes 4 to 6 servings.

Accompaniments

This chapter contains some basic recipes and some recipes for sauces and side dishes that go well with loaves of all kinds. Many of the recipes start with a basic recipe and then give several variations, so be sure to try them all.

I've included a recipe here for cooking dried beans, because so many of the recipes, especially in the Vegetable Loaves chapter, are made with beans. If you cook your own beans, they taste fresher, are less expensive, and contain less sodium than canned beans.

Basic Cooked Beans

Cooked beans freeze well but should not be refrigerated for more than two or three days.

1 pound dried beans such as navy, black, pinto, or red beans
About 6 cups water
1 teaspoon salt

Pick over beans and remove any discolored beans or small rocks. Rinse beans. Place beans in a large bowl or saucepan and add enough water to cover by about 1 inch. Let stand overnight. Or cover beans with water, bring to a boil, and boil 5 minutes. Let stand 1 hour. Drain soaked beans.

Place drained beans in a large saucepan. Add the 6 cups water and bring to a boil. Boil 10 minutes. Reduce heat, cover, and simmer until beans are beginning to soften. Add salt and cook until beans are tender, about 1-1/2 hours depending on the type and age of the beans. Add more water as needed during cooking.

Serve as a side dish or drain and use in any recipe calling for cooked or canned beans. Makes about 5 cups.

Variation

Add 1 small chopped onion, 1 garlic clove, 1 bay leaf, and 1 parsley sprig to beans during cooking. Discard bay leaf and parsley before serving.

Black Bean & White Corn Salad

Beans and corn are a traditional combination, and this one features my favorites—
black beans and white corn.

2 cups cooked black beans or 1 (15-oz.) can black beans, drained and rinsed
1 (10-oz.) package white corn, thawed and drained
1/2 cup finely chopped red onion
1/2 cup finely chopped green bell pepper
2 tablespoons chopped flat-leaf parsley
1/2 tablespoon chopped basil or 1/2 teaspoon dried leaf basil
1/4 cup olive oil
1 tablespoon balsamic vinegar
2 tablespoons seasoned rice vinegar
Salt and freshly ground pepper

Combine beans, corn, onion, bell pepper, parsley, and basil in a medium-size bowl. Combine olive oil and vinegars in a small bowl; whisk to combine. Pour dressing over salad and toss to combine. Season with salt and pepper. Makes 4 servings.

Guiltless Onion Rings

I got the idea for these one day when I purchased some wonderful large Vidalia onions that were perfect for onion rings. However, we were trying to cut down on calories, so I decided to bake the onion rings instead of frying them.

1 (1-lb.) Vidalia or other sweet onion
1/2 cup all-purpose flour
1/2 teaspoon chili powder
1/4 teaspoon red (cayenne) pepper
Salt and freshly ground pepper

Preheat oven to 350°F (175°C). Spray a baking sheet with nonstick cooking spray. Cut onion crosswise into thin slices. Soak in ice water 20 minutes. Pat almost dry with paper towels.

Combine flour, chili powder, cayenne, salt, and pepper in a plastic bag. Add onion rings in batches and shake to lightly coat. Shake off excess flour.

Arrange onions on baking sheet. Lightly spray with nonstick cooking spray. Bake 40 minutes, turning after 20 minutes. Makes 2 servings.

Potatoes on the Grill

Prepare these any time that you have extra room on the grill, or cook in the oven.

1 large russet potato, unpeeled, thinly sliced
1 large green bell pepper, thinly sliced
2 tablespoons olive oil
1 teaspoon dried leaf oregano
1/2 teaspoon dried red chile flakes or to taste
Salt and freshly ground pepper

Preheat grill. Tear off two large sheets of heavy-duty foil. Spray insides with nonstick cooking spray.

Add potatoes and bell pepper to a large bowl. Add olive oil, oregano, chile flakes, salt, and pepper. Toss to coat with oil. Divide mixture between foil sheets. Fold edges over and seal tightly.

Place packages on grill and cook, turning about every 5 minutes, for about 20 minutes, depending on heat, or until potatoes are tender. Makes 4 servings.

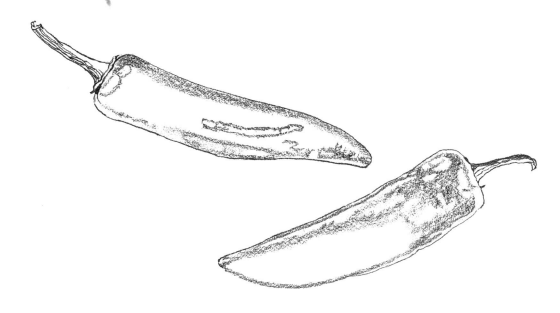

Mashed Potatoes

Mashed potatoes are one of the favorite side dishes to serve with meatloaf.

2 pounds potatoes
1/4 cup butter or margarine or to taste, softened
Milk
Salt and freshly ground pepper
Freshly grated nutmeg

Peel potatoes, if desired. Cut into 1-1/2-inch pieces. Cook in boiling salted water until tender, about 20 minutes. Drain potatoes and return to heat to dry 1 or 2 minutes, shaking pan to prevent sticking.

Mash potatoes. Stir in butter and enough milk to make a soft consistency. Season with salt, pepper, and nutmeg. Makes 4 servings.

Variations
Roasted Garlic Potatoes
Preheat oven to 375°F (190°C). Wrap a garlic head in foil. Roast about 45 minutes or until garlic is soft. Squeeze cloves out of skin and mash. Add to mashed potatoes.

Herbed Potatoes
Mince 1 to 3 tablespoons fresh herbs of your choice or add 1 teaspoon to 1 tablespoon dried herbs (depending on flavor of herb). Good choices include dill, basil, thyme, savory, chives, parsley, and rosemary or a combination.

Buttermilk Herbed Potatoes
Substitute buttermilk or yogurt for regular milk. Add minced herbs.

Green Potatoes
Cook 2 ounces arugula or 4 to 6 ounces spinach or rapini until crisp-tender. Finely chop and add to potatoes along with two or three roasted garlic cloves.

Cheesy Potatoes

Stir in 4 ounces (1 cup shredded) of your favorite cheese such as Cheddar, Gouda, or Swiss or two ounces (1/2 cup) of crumbled blue or grated Parmesan cheese.

Sour Cream Potatoes

Substitute sour cream for butter and milk. Stir in 2 tablespoons each minced chives and parsley.

Baked Mashed Potatoes

Preheat oven to 400°F (205°C). Grease a baking dish. Add a little additional milk to mashed potatoes and beat until fluffy. Spoon potatoes into baking dish and sprinkle with 1/4 cup grated Parmesan cheese. Bake until golden brown.

Creamy Potatoes

Substitute 3 ounces light or regular cream cheese for butter.

Caramelized Onion & Potatoes

Cook 1 thinly sliced large sweet onion, covered, in a large skillet over very low heat until onion turns golden brown (do not burn). Stir into mashed potatoes.

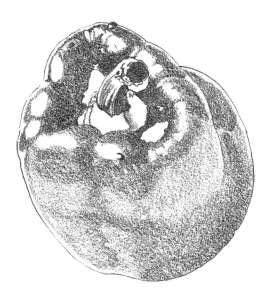

Oven-Roasted Potato Wedges

Delicious and moist on the inside and brown and crispy on the outside.

2 pounds medium-size white rose potatoes
2 tablespoons olive oil
Salt and freshly ground pepper
1/2 teaspoon dried dill weed or 1/2 teaspoon dried rosemary

Place potatoes in a medium-size saucepan. Add enough water to come halfway up potatoes and bring to a boil. Reduce heat, cover, and simmer until potatoes are almost tender, about 20 minutes. Drain potatoes and cool slightly.

Preheat oven to 350°F (175°C). Cut potatoes into wedges. Place in a baking pan and drizzle with oil. Season with salt and pepper. Toss gently to coat with oil.

Bake, turning about every 15 minutes, until browned on all sides, about 40 minutes. Sprinkle with herbs near end of baking time and toss to combine. Makes about 6 servings.

Fresh Tomato Sauce

Make this in summer, when vine-ripened tomatoes are available.

About 2 pounds fresh tomatoes
1 tablespoon olive oil
1 small onion, very finely chopped
1 garlic clove, minced
1 tablespoon chopped fresh flat-leaf parsley
1 tablespoon chopped fresh basil or 1 teaspoon dried leaf basil
1 teaspoon chopped fresh oregano or 1/4 teaspoon dried leaf oregano
Salt and freshly ground pepper

Peel tomatoes and finely chop; place in a medium-size bowl.

Heat oil in a medium-size saucepan over medium-low heat. Add onion and garlic and sauté until softened, but not browned.

Add hot onion mixture, parsley, basil, oregano, salt, and pepper to tomatoes; toss to combine. Let stand at room temperature about 30 minutes for flavors to blend. Makes about 5 cups.

 Note

To quickly peel tomatoes, drop them into a pan of boiling water about 1 minute. Remove with a slotted spoon and place in ice water to cool quickly.

Easy Tomato Sauce

Vary the herbs to match the loaf. Quick to prepare, this will soon become a favorite for pasta, also.

2 tablespoons olive oil
1 cup finely chopped onion
1 large garlic clove, minced
1 (28-oz.) can crushed tomatoes in puree
1 teaspoon dried leaf herbs such as oregano, basil, or marjoram
Freshly ground pepper

Heat oil in a medium-size saucepan over medium-low heat. Add onion and garlic and sauté until softened but not browned. Add tomatoes, herbs, and pepper. Simmer about 10 minutes. Serve hot over your favorite loaf. Makes about 3-1/2 cups.

Variation

Cooked Fresh Tomato Sauce

Substitute about 2-1/2 pounds chopped plum tomatoes for canned tomatoes. Simmer sauce about 25 minutes or until thickened. Season with salt to taste. For a smooth sauce, press through a sieve with a wooden spoon.

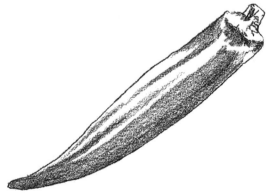

Mango-Tomatillo Salsa

Very versatile, this goes especially well with chicken loaves.

1 ripe mango, peeled and finely chopped
8 ounces tomatillos, finely chopped
1/4 cup finely chopped cilantro
1 jalapeño chile, minced
1/8 teaspoon salt
Fresh lime juice

Combine mango, tomatillos, cilantro, chile, salt, and lime juice to taste in a bowl. Let stand 30 minutes before serving. Makes 4 servings.

Variation

Process all ingredients in a blender or food processor until almost smooth.

Note

Remove the papery coverings from the tomatillos and rinse with hot water to remove the sticky resin.

Basic White Sauce (Béchamel Sauce)

For other sauces based on this classic, see variations below.

2 tablespoons butter or margarine
2 tablespoons all-purpose flour
2 cups regular or low-fat milk
Pinch of freshly grated nutmeg
Salt and freshly ground white pepper

Melt butter in top of a double boiler over low heat. Stir in flour and cook, stirring, about 3 minutes. Whisk in milk and cook, whisking constantly, until blended. Increase heat to medium-low and cook, whisking constantly, until mixture comes to a boil.

Place top of double boiler over simmering water and cook sauce, stirring occasionally, about 30 minutes. Add nutmeg, salt, and white pepper. Thin to desired consistency with additional milk, if needed. Makes about 1-1/2 cups.

Variations

Cheese Sauce
Stir 1 cup shredded Cheddar cheese or other hard cheese into hot sauce; stir until cheese melts.

Blue Cheese Sauce
Stir in 1/4 cup crumbled blue cheese and 1/4 teaspoon dried leaf thyme into hot sauce.

Dill Sauce
Stir 1/4 cup finely chopped dill and 1 tablespoon fresh lemon juice into hot sauce.

Onion Sauce
Sauté 1 cup finely chopped onion in 1 tablespoon butter or margarine over low heat until softened. Stir into hot sauce. Season with hot pepper sauce.

Leek Sauce

Melt 1 tablespoon butter in a large skillet over low heat. Add 2 chopped leeks and 1/4 cup chopped parsley and cook, covered, about 20 minutes or until leeks are softened. Stir leek mixture and 1 tablespoon fresh lemon juice into hot sauce.

Note

If you don't have a double boiler, transfer the sauce to a heatproof bowl and place over a large saucepan of simmering water.

Papaya-Jicama Salsa

Melon can be substituted for the papaya.

2 cups diced papaya
1 cup diced jicama
1 serrano chile, minced
2 green onions, minced
1/4 teaspoon salt
Fresh lemon juice

Combine papaya, jicama, chile, onions, salt, and lemon juice to taste in a small bowl. Let stand 30 minutes before serving. Makes 4 servings.

Variation

For a mild salsa, substitute 1/2 cup chopped red bell pepper for the serrano chile.

Metric Conversion Charts

Comparison to Metric Measure

When You Know	Symbol	Multiply By	To Find	Symbol
teaspoons	tsp	5.0	milliliters	ml
tablespoons	tbsp	15.0	milliliters	ml
fluid ounces	fl. oz.	30.0	milliliters	ml
cups	c.	0.24	liters	l
pints	pt.	0.47	liters	l
quarts	qt.	0.95	liters	l
ounces	oz.	28.0	grams	g
pounds	lb.	0.45	kilograms	kg
Fahrenheit	F	5/9 (after subtracting 32)	Celsius	C

Liquid Measure to Milliliters

1/4 teaspoon	=	1.25 milliliters
1/2 teaspoon	=	2.5 milliliters
3/4 teaspoon	=	3.75 milliliters
1 teaspoon	=	5.0 milliliters
1-1/4 teaspoons	=	6.25 milliliters
1-1/2 teaspoons	=	7.5 milliliters
1-3/4 teaspoons	=	8.75 milliliters
2 teaspoons	=	10.0 milliliters
1 tablespoon	=	15.0 milliliters
2 tablespoons	=	30.0 milliliters

Fahrenheit to Celsius

F	C
200-205	95
220-225	105
245-250	120
275	135
300-305	150
325-330	165
345-350	175
370-375	190
400-405	205
425-530	220
445-450	230
470-475	245
500	260

Liquid Measure to Liters

1/4 cup	=	0.06 liters
1/2 cup	=	0.12 liters
3/4 cup	=	0.18 liters
1 cup	=	0.24 liters
1-1/4 cups	=	0.3 liters
1-1/2 cups	=	0.36 liters
2 cups	=	0.48 liters
2-1/2 cups	=	0.6 liters
3 cups	=	0.72 liters
3-1/2 cups	=	0.84 liters
4 cups	=	0.96 liters
4-1/2 cups	=	1.08 liters
5 cups	=	1.2 liters
5-1/2 cups	=	1.32 liters

Index